2001-02

EDITORS:
Sidney Gottlieb and Richard Allen

FOUNDING EDITOR:
Christopher Brookhouse

COVER DESIGN: Deborah Dutko

The *Hitchcock Annual* (ISSN 1062-5518) is published each autumn. Editorial, subscription, and advertising correspondence should be addressed to: Sidney Gottlieb, Editor, *Hitchcock Annual*, English Department, Sacred Heart University, Fairfield, CT 06432-1000. E-mail address: spgottlieb@aol.com

Single copies of each volume cost $12.00 plus postage for individuals. The rate for continuing subscribers is $10.00 per volume for individuals and $25.00 for institutions; outside the U.S. add $3.00 for postage. All checks should be payable to: *Hitchcock Annual*. Inquire about the availability of back issues and offprints of individual articles.

We invite articles on all aspects of Hitchcock and his work, and encourage a variety of approaches, methods, and viewpoints. For all submissions, please follow the guidelines of the *Chicago Manual of Style*, and include two copies of the essay to be considered (only one of which will be returned) with return postage. Decision time is normally three to four months. Upon acceptance, contributors will be asked to submit their work on computer disk (IBM-compatible). The responsibility for securing any permissions required for publishing material in the essay or related illustrations rests with the author.

The *Hitchcock Annual* is indexed in the *Film Literature Index and MLA International Bibliography*.

HITCHCOCK ANNUAL
2001–02

GUS VAN SANT VS. ALFRED HITCHCOCK:
A *PSYCHO* DOSSIER

BOOK REVIEWS

Editors' Notes

In 1990, when I found myself with the time and financial support to start the *Hitchcock Annual*, I wrote to Lesley Brill, Leonard Leff, Leland Poague, and Kristin Thompson, all of whom I knew only through their work, to ask if they would serve on the editorial board. Much to my surprise and delight, they agreed. The other original member was my former colleague Margaret O'Connor. Eventually Diane Carson brought her critical perspective to the group. In later issues, Loring Silet took up the burden of the book review section, for which I am extremely grateful.

Sid Gottlieb phoned me before the first issue appeared. He introduced himself and spoke of his keen interest in Hitchcock, as well as his experience editing and publishing a scholarly journal on George Herbert. Every issue of the *Annual* after the first one has been laid out and set and sent to the printer by Sid. Eventually Sid also took on more and more of the editorial work.

The *Hitchcock Annual* would not have prospered without the unselfish work of the above-named members of the editorial staff. I recall only once when anyone declined to read a submission, and to do so promptly. Not only were the readers' comments helpful to me, but also to the authors, whose work the readers inevitably improved by their suggestions. In a time when book and journal editing is often uncaring, our editorial board stood out for its thoughtfulness and dedication, and their efforts have helped shape each issue. As I step down as editor, I want to thank them one last time, and hold their efforts up as a model as Sid and Richard Allen make what I expect will be a smooth transition and take the *Hitchcock Annual* into its second decade.

Christopher Brookhouse

We are grateful to Chris Brookhouse for starting the *Hitchcock Annual* and maintaining it at such a high level for so many years, and are very excited about the challenges and responsibilities facing us as he places the journal in our hands. Our goals are in most respects basically the same as his, and there will undoubtedly be a strong sense of continuity between what the journal has been and what it will become. At the same time, we envision ourselves as the custodians of an enterprise that will grow, expand, and develop in ways that we can hardly predict. We have high expectations as we relaunch a journal devoted to the work of a figure who looms large in the history of audio-visual media, and whose work has long been pivotal in debates about the nature of film and how the medium should be understood.

We would like to reaffirm that the *Hitchcock Annual* seeks to publish the best and liveliest in Hitchcock criticism and scholarship, aimed at an audience not limited to specialists in film studies. We welcome essays from all theoretical and critical perspectives, including interpretive analyses focusing on particular texts as well as historical or cultural studies of the director's *oeuvre* and career. We also invite essays examining the cultural and textual influences on Hitchcock's film and television work, and the reception and impact of his work upon directors, critics, and theorists worldwide. To help make the journal a repository of vital material relevant to understanding and appreciating Hitchcock, we aim to regularly print rare documents by and interviews with Hitchcock or people he worked with, and translations of key essays on Hitchcock otherwise unavailable in English. Finally, each volume will review current work on Hitchcock, and occasionally (as in the current volume) include critical exchanges.

We will complete the transition in the next volume with the announcement of our expanded editorial board, one dedicated to the labors of love and rigor so well described by Chris Brookhouse in his valedictory note that we hope will always define the *Hitchcock Annual*.

Sidney Gottlieb and Richard Allen

WORKING WITH HITCH:
A SCREENWRITER'S FORUM WITH EVAN HUNTER, ARTHUR LAURENTS, AND JOSEPH STEFANO

Edited by WALTER SREBNICK

Arthur Laurents, screenwriter of *Rope* (1948), Joseph Stefano, who wrote *Psycho* (1960), and Evan Hunter, who wrote *The Birds* (1963), appeared together on a panel at the 1999 New York University Hitchcock Centennial Celebration to discuss their collaboration with Alfred Hitchcock. They had never met or discussed working with Hitchcock before this event. Hunter and Stefano had both worked on earlier drafts of *Marnie* (1963), although neither was aware of the other's involvement. The following is essentially a verbatim transcript of their conversation with each other and the audience. Slight editorial changes have been made only in the interest of clarity or grammatical and syntactical coherence. Special thanks to Rahul Hamid for transcribing the tape of this session.

Arthur Laurents has been known as a playwright and stage director, as well as a screenwriter, for more than fifty years. Born in Brooklyn, New York, in 1918, Laurents began his career writing for radio. Among his best known stage plays and musicals are *Home of the Brave* (1945), *The Bird Cage* (1950), *The Time of the Cuckoo* (1952), *A Clearing in the Woods* (1957), *West Side Story* (1957), *Gypsy* (1959), and *Hallelujah, Baby!* (1967). In addition to *Rope*, his screenplays include: *The Snake Pit* (1948), *Caught* (1949), *Anastasia* (1956), *Bonjour Tristesse* (1958), *The Way We Were* (1973), and *The Turning Point* (1977). In 2000, he published a memoir, *Original Story By: A Memoir of Broadway and Hollywood* (Knopf).

Born in 1922 in South Philadelphia, Joseph Stefano began his career as a performer on the musical stage and as a songwriter before turning to film and television. In addition to *Psycho*, he has written the screenplays for *The Black Orchid* (1959), *The Naked Edge* (1961), *Eye of the Cat* (1969), *Futz*

(1969), *Blackout* (1989), *Psycho IV* (1991), and *Two Bits* (1995). His original screenplay for *Psycho* was used virtually intact in Gus Van Sant's 1998 remake, and he received screenplay credit for it. He has also worked extensively as a writer and a producer on television, and was the original writer/producer of *The Outer Limits* (1963-64).

Evan Hunter was born in 1926 in New York City. Known principally as a novelist for such works as *The Blackboard Jungle* (1954), *Strangers When We Meet* (1958), *Mothers and Daughters* (1961), *Last Summer* (1969), *Sons* (1969), *Walk Proud* (1979), *Love Dad* (1981), *Lizzie* (1984), and *Privileged Conversation* (1996), he is also the author of more than fifty 87th Precinct novels under his pseudonym, Ed McBain, and more than a dozen Matthew Hope novels. In addition to *The Birds*, he has written screenplays for *Strangers When We Meet* (1960), *Fuzz* (1972), and *Walk Proud* (1979), as well as plays and television shows, including episodes of *Alfred Hitchcock Presents*. He has written a memoir of his experience with Hitchcock, *Me and Hitch* (Faber and Faber, 1997).

SREBNICK: We all have heard how deeply involved Hitchcock was in the creation of screenplays. In fact, a recent *Sight and Sound* article argues that what makes Hitchcock unique is not his suspense or visual style, but his particular combination of the verbal and the visual, even the tension between the two. With that in mind, just what was Hitchcock's contribution to the writing process on your film? How much control did he exercise? How specific was he in laying out scenes? Did you feel that visual or technical considerations overwhelmed narrative ones? Was there a signature writing style or writing practice for Hitchcock, and did it differ from how you worked with other directors? I'll begin with Mr. Laurents.

LAURENTS: I can answer that in one minute. Hitchcock had nothing to do with the writing. He wasn't very interested in it, and that's because *Rope* was an aberrant picture. I don't think it was a very good idea of how to make a picture; it was a stunt. And I hesitate, because I've just finished my memoir, which is going to be published soon. I wish I had it here. I could just read it to you and make it easier. Anyway, *Rope* came from an English play called *Rope's End* by Patrick Hamilton, and Hitch decided to shoot it as a play, which is why there was no interference. All he was concerned with was this trick of no cuts, that each take was as long as a reel. If you have the questionable fortune to see the picture, it's very obvious. The camera comes in on somebody's back while they quickly change the film.

My job was to make this English play American. The play is basically about the Leopold-Loeb murders, which nobody mentioned and nobody admitted. It dealt with these two homosexual boys and their homosexual teacher, which nobody also admitted. Nobody said the word "homosexual"; it was referred to as "it" by Hitch, by the studio, by everyone. They just pretended it wasn't there, but they wanted it there. So, actually translating that English play into an American play, being aware of "it" wasn't as easy as I thought it would be because the English use a lot of expressions which sent the censors up the wall. Hitch's producer was a man named Sidney Bernstein, an Englishman, a very nice man. He said, "I want every word to be a literary gem." Well, I thought I was writing a movie, not a literary piece. Since my work was done before the shooting began, I returned to New York after finishing the screenplay. So while I was gone, Sidney restored a lot of the British locutions I had cut, such as the phrase "my dear boy." And everyone of those "my dear boys" went to the censor who said, "homosexual dialogue, out!"

And when they came to shooting the picture, Hitch wanted Cary Grant, Montgomery Clift, and Farley Granger to play the principal characters. He got Farley but he told me Cary Grant and Montgomery Clift were afraid to do it because of their own questionable sexuality, or how it was perceived. So they got Jimmy Stewart, who has no sexuality, which posed a little problem for the picture. Nobody knew that he was supposed to have had a "relationship" with these boys.

Hitch was a delightful man to be with. He was consumed with this technical stunt, and we only had two disagreements about the film. One was about these two boys serving dinner on a chest in which there may be a body. Well, after the picture was finished, he shot the murder and put the body inside, which I thought was a mistake because it destroyed suspense. The other was that although the boy was strangled, he wanted somebody to knock over a bottle of red wine on the white tablecloth on the chest so it would spill and you would think it was blood. I said that if the victim was strangled there would be no blood. He wasn't very pleased with that. But he took out the red wine and concentrated on a lot of shots of rope tied around some books.

Obviously, I'm not very wild about the movie, but I had a wonderful time working with him. I don't know how it was with Evan or Joe—in my day, at any rate, when he liked you, you became part of his family. And you were invited to a family dinner, which consisted of himself, his wife Alma, his daughter Pat, his friend Ingrid Bergman, his other friend Cary Grant, and guests like that.

Well, I went and was busy writing home about it to my mother like mad. We became very good friends, and when the picture was finished, he gave me a novel to read called *Under Capricorn*, which I didn't think much of. I thought we were friends and I could tell him how I felt about it. But when I did, he cut me off. And he never spoke to me again until some years passed and he handed me something called *Torn Curtain*. I didn't like that either, and he didn't speak to me for a while again. The third and last time he contacted me was about *Topaz*, which I also didn't like. I live a lot of the time on the beach, and my neighbor then was a relative of Jules Stein, who owned MCA and Universal, I think. Anyway, Hitch was visiting them, and this time he asked me why I didn't think *Topaz* would make a good picture. We talked and it was pleasant, but he was never really friendly again. I think if you rejected his ideas, he felt you rejected him. End.

SREBNICK: I don't think it's truly the end. I think you are going to get some specific questions in a little while. Thank you. Mr. Stefano?

STEFANO: As far as writing a screenplay for Alfred Hitchcock, I was totally amazed at how much independence I had. When I first met him, we started having meetings every day, and he was not the least bit interested in what the characters would say or why they would say it. He wanted no background from me in any way. He just wanted to talk about how the movie was going to be filmed. He was totally visual. If I asked him any questions about the characters, his response was usually "What do you want the audience to think?" or "What do you want the audience to feel?" I perceived early on that the audience was the third person in that room and that we were both kind of slaves to that person. It was an interesting experience because he included me in the actual structure and architecture of the picture so that we both knew every moment what was going on. This went on for about four or five weeks, meeting every day. Most of the time we talked about my morning psychoanalysis sessions. He was very interested in them. It seemed to me that he never met a person before who announced he was in psychoanalysis.

LAURENTS: I told him I was in it too.

STEFANO: He wanted to know what was going on there, and one day I went in and said that I realized that day that the reason I was going to write a fabulous Norman Bates was that I learned while lying on the couch that I would have gladly killed my mother on at least three occasions. He was very shocked and thought it was wonderful and that it would certainly help the movie. That was about it. I went home and wrote.

We had in all, I think, two arguments. One had to do with the budget. I wanted the camera to pull all the way up to the ceiling when Martin Balsam is coming up the stairs about to be stabbed. I wanted this so that we wouldn't know we weren't seeing mother. Instead we'd see her come out from way above and we'd see her wig. If we were on the landing with the two of them, we would ask "Why aren't we seeing her face?" So he finally said it would cost us $25,000 more to build this thing up on the ceiling of the sound stage, and I didn't blink because to me if you're going to make a movie, you're going to spend $25,000 to do it right. So he agreed finally, and the only other question he had was the fear that the psychiatrist coming in at the end to explain the story would be a "hat grabber," to use his term for it. And I said I didn't think anybody was going to be grabbing their hats at that point in the movie and leaving the theater. In the novel the sister and Marion's lover kind of theorize about what it would mean, that this young man was wearing a wig when he came in to kill her. I felt that they had no right theorizing about what had happened and we had better tell the audience what had gone on. So he finally agreed to the psychiatrist and that was it.

Then I went home, wrote the script, brought it back and gave it to him. He came in the next day and said that Alma loved it. That was it: that was all he ever said. Then he asked me to change one word and I said "No." Well, first I said, "Is that wrong for the character? You think the character wouldn't use the word 'lurid'?" And he said, "I don't think it's wrong." And I said, "What do you think he would say: 'We'll write each other dirty love letters' or 'sexy love letters' or 'pornographic love letters'?" I liked lurid and he said, "Well, it's a word I hate." I said, "Well, I don't think we should take it out based on that." So it stayed in. He left it in. I found him very amenable to just about anything regarding characters and dialogue.

I gave him a script when we stared production in which I had bracketed lines that I thought could go if we were running overtime. And mainly he shot those lines and then cut them in the cutting room. But it was probably the best experience of my life because until then I had written only one movie and one television show and wanted to work with somebody who could teach me how to make movies. I had seen all of his movies, and on days when he wasn't actually up to working or to talking I'd ask him if I could see *Under Capricorn*, for instance, or *Vertigo* or any of the movies, all of which I had already seen. And then I would come back in and ask him questions. "Why did you do this? And why did you choose this moment to expose the fact that this woman in *Vertigo* had also been the one in the beginning?" It was interesting because he was incredibly generous and very giving. He would draw diagrams for me of how he had gotten certain shots in certain movies. He gave me an education that was fantastic because there was no AFI in those days. It was a wonderful way to make a movie, and I thoroughly enjoyed it and remember most of it.

SREBNICK: Thank you. Mr. Hunter?

HUNTER: I entered Hitch's creative life when he was looking for a respectability which he felt had eluded him. I remember being in his office on the first day. There was a long corridor in his office, and one wall was entirely filled with all the awards he had won all over the world and all the honors he had received. I got in a little earlier that morning than he did and I was having a cup of coffee when he came in and I said, "Good morning, that's quite a collection you got here, Hitch." And he looked at it kind of sadly, nodded, and said, "Always a bridesmaid never a bride." He was referring, of course, to the fact that he had never received an Academy Award.

I had done some stuff for *Alfred Hitchcock Presents*, and when the call from Hitch came and he asked me if I wanted to do *The Birds* (I had already met him prior to that), he told me immediately on the phone that we were going to throw out the story. He said, "Forget it, we're only going to stay with the notion of birds attacking people, that and the title. And that is it, so you'd better come out here with some ideas." Thus freed of the burden of having to respect someone else's work, I went out with some ideas and he had some ideas, and we shot them down. In the first week of working together, we explored all the ideas and shot them down on both sides and started from scratch. The process was that I would come in to the studio each morning. We would sit down, just the two of us, with Hitch in a big wing-back chair with his hands on his belly and his feet barely touching the floor. He was always dressed immaculately in a dark suit with a white shirt and a dark tie, black shoes and socks. I would start winging the story at him, and he would listen. By the end of the day, I would go back home and type up what we had discussed the day before, and the next day when I'd come in he'd say, "Tell me the story so far." I would tell him the story so far, which was easy in the beginning but got a little more difficult as we went along.

We never ever once discussed camera angles or the pictorial aspect of the film. I asked him at the beginning of the film, "Do you want me to call the shots?" A lot of directors just like the master shot and they'll do it themselves, but a lot of directors like you to call each shot: the close shots, the wide shots, and the two shots and all of it. He said, "Yes, I want you to call every shot in the movie." And I did so in the script, which, incidentally, he went very far away from when he was doing the actual shooting.

He would ask surprising questions. I would be in the middle of telling the story so far and he would say, "Has she called her father yet?" I'd say, "What?" "The girl, has she called her father?" And I'd say, "No." "Well, she's been away from San Francisco overnight. Does he know where she is? Has she called to tell him she's staying in this town?" I said, "No." And he said, "Don't you think she should call him?" I said, "Yes, you know it's not a difficult thing to have a person pick up the phone." Questions like that.

I don't know if you recall the movie. There's a scene where after this massive bird attack on the house Mitch, the male character, is asleep in a chair and Melanie hears something. She takes a flashlight and she goes up to investigate, and this leads to the big scene in the attic where all the birds attack her. I was telling him about this scene and he was listening very intently, and then he said, "Let me see if I understand this correctly. There has been a massive attack on the house and they have boarded it up and Mitch is asleep and she hears a sound and she goes to investigate?" I said, "Well, yes," and he said, "Is she daft? Why doesn't she wake him up?" And I said, "Well, he's very tired." He said, "Well, we'll take the curse off it. Here's what we'll do. We'll have her first look at the love birds and see that they're all right. Then, we'll have her check several rooms along the way to see that everything's all right before she opens that door where the attack comes." As a matter of fact this isn't the way he did it in the film. She just goes right upstairs and opens the door. That was one of his concerns: that we lull the viewers into a sort of complacency before we bam them with a shock.

The question he asked over and over again was "Why are the birds doing it?" We struggled with this one for a long, long time: Why are the birds doing it? We came up with a hundred reasons for them doing it and they either sounded like science fiction or the supernatural, and we didn't want to do that kind of movie. We decided that we were not going to explain it. There was a scene he never shot where both Melanie and Mitch are outside discussing the bird attacks after the attack down the chimney by the finches. They discuss the problem and try to find some solution to it. They also discuss it in the scene in the Tides restaurant when the bird expert, Mrs. Bundy, comes in. But we never ever tried to explain why they were attacking, and we felt it would be a more meaningful way to go instead of inventing reasons for bird attacks.

He was constantly concerned about Melanie's character, constantly trying to pin her down. In the early days, we were struggling to find an approach to the film. We were then still at Paramount Studios before we moved over to Universal. I went out for lunch one day (he used to take the lunch hour, I should explain, to confer with his secretaries and various other people who came in on projects that had nothing to do with *The Birds*, because he was running a vast enterprise there), and I was walking around the lot and I had an idea. I came back and I said, ''Why don't we do a screwball comedy that turns to terror?'' It appealed to him; he liked that idea.

He had a marvelous sense of humor. He would interrupt story conferences every day to tell another anecdote about one thing or another. He was a joy to work with. He liked that idea and we started from there. We started building the concept of a madcap heiress who played practical jokes and got involved with this guy who she's immediately smitten with. As in the great screwball comedies, they meet and they argue all the time until they realize they both love each other madly. That was the concept. We built it toward that end, but he kept having doubts about the character. He kept trying to finds ways to give her a more solid base than the person I intended her to be and which I thought he agreed she should be. As the film progressed, and as I learned later that he was showing it to other writers all over the lot and trying to beef up the character of the girl, she began doing things that seemed to me out of character. That's another story.

To answer the question, he was involved in it not toward creating a story but more by way of editing the story; more by way of questioning every twist and turn the plot took; questioning character motivation in every scene; questioning the relationship between Mitch and Annie, the other woman in his life; questioning the relationship between him and his mother—how his mother would react to this sophisticated woman coming from San Francisco. When I started writing it, he would call the house to inform my wife, for example, that a fire was raging in Bel Air in his backyard, or call her to ask if she had finally found a hairdresser, or a place where she could take tennis lessons. He never called me while I was working on it, never once, and never once asked her how the script was going—never, never, never. He would take us to dinner, and take us to the racetrack. He would entertain us lavishly in his home and elsewhere, but he never once asked how the script was going. When I finished it, I delivered it and he gave me notes on it and I rewrote it. I came back to New York, and he called and said he needed a scene where they try to explain it all. I wrote the scene in the Tides restaurant, which I still feel is the best scene in the movie. It's like a one-act play, writing-wise. There are many brilliant scenes pictorially. That was it; that was the extent of our relationship. While he was shooting *The Birds*, I began working on *Marnie*.

SREBNICK: Didn't you also work on an earlier draft of *Marnie*, Mr. Stefano?

STEFANO: Yes. Hitch called me one day and told me that Grace Kelly wanted to make a movie for him. He had a book called *Marnie* that he thought would be a very good movie. He sent it to me. I liked a lot of it and pictured Grace Kelly very easily playing it. Then he said to me that he felt Miss Kelly would not want to read the book. (Actually, she was more than Miss Kelly at that point.) He said that I should write a very detailed treatment of the movie and we would send it to her. That would be close to a screenplay, and she would have a better idea of what was expected of her. So we discussed it in much the same way as I mentioned about working on *Psycho*. We spent mornings together and afternoons and dreamed up this movie without much reference to the book, although I did stay pretty close to it. Shortly before I finished the treatment (about two weeks later), he called and told me that Miss Kelly had changed her mind. Apparently, she and her husband had gotten the money they needed elsewhere. So she wasn't going to make a movie. I thought that there were a lot of very wonderful actresses who also could play this part, but he was royally pissed off. He said that he had no interest in doing it with anybody else. Later, when he decided to use Tippi Hedren, I was then producing *The Outer Limits* on television and didn't even know that he was going to do it. There was no way I could have gotten out of my contract with ABC. So that was the last I heard of it until I heard that the movie was going to be made with Tippi Hedren.

HUNTER: He never showed me Joe's treatment, and I understand—Jay [Presson Allen] can corroborate this—that he never showed Jay my script when she replaced me on the project. I just read the novel. It was a book by Winston Graham, and it was a pretty good suspense novel—actually what we now call a thriller, as opposed to a mystery. I said, "Yes, I'd like to do it." While we were shooting *The Birds* up in Bodega Bay, I flew to San Francisco and we had several meetings, which is how I happened to be on the set. Directors do not like writers on the set. Directors don't like writers. We discussed *Marnie*. But there was a scene in the book that bothered me. I told him about that at our first meeting on it. I said that I didn't think I wanted to write that scene. He said, "Don't worry we'll talk about that later— don't worry about it." Contrary to not worrying about it, it kept coming up again, and again, and again.

The scene takes place (I don't know how many of you have seen the film) on Marnie's wedding night. The Sean Connery character rapes Marnie. (This was not Sean Connery at the time. This was just a character named Mark Rutland. Sean was not even in anybody's mind for the part.) He approaches her, while she is just cowering in the corner and terrified. She's frigid. This is part of her psychiatric profile. It's obvious she's not being coy or seductive. She's terrified, and he rapes her. I said to Hitch, "I'm not sure I can recover this character ever again after this moment. I think he's lost to every woman in the audience." He said, "No." He wanted that scene in the film.

I went home and I wrote two drafts. I wrote one draft the way Hitch wanted it with the rape. I'm pretty good at rape scenes, but usually my rapists are not supposed to be sympathetic characters. I wrote the other scene the way I thought it should go, where he comforts her and says "Don't worry we'll work this out." The mistake I made was that I put the rape scene on yellow pages outside of the script and

I put my way on white pages in the script. I wrote a long letter to Hitch explaining why I thought my way was a better way to go and that I was certain once he had read my way that he would realize it was the way to go and we could forget all this silly nonsense about a rape. Well, I got fired. Jay will again corroborate that. When she and I were discussing this years later she said, "Evan, the minute you told Hitch that you did not want to write that rape scene, you bought your ticket back to New York. The only reason he wanted to make that movie was the rape scene."

LAURENTS: May I interject something here?

HUNTER: Please.

LAURENTS: I was listening to you and to Joe, and there's one element that I think is very dominant in Hitchcock in all three pictures, *Marnie*, *Psycho* and *Rope*. He was fascinated by sexual kinkiness. It was almost an obsession with him. Here you tell how he wanted to have a rape scene, and in *Psycho* you have a murder in drag, and I wrote this picture with two homosexuals under the influence of a third who commit a murder for a thrill. He talked about it all the time, to me anyway. I think it influenced his work a great deal.

HUNTER: The interesting thing about *The Birds* is that there's hardly a kiss in the film. It's antiseptic. It's a totally antiseptic film.

LAURENTS: Yes, well they get their eyes pecked out.

HUNTER: That's true. I always find that very sexy—having my eyes pecked out.

LAURENTS: I didn't say "sex." I said "kink."

STEFANO: Well, as we all know, there certainly wasn't any kink in *Psycho*!

HUNTER: Actually, I intended Mrs. Bundy to be the sex object in *The Birds*.

SREBNICK: One issue, I think, that this raises is the relationship of the screenplay to the original source. Mr. Laurents, if I understand you correctly, you think that *Rope* was a sort of slavish attempt to remake the stage play?

LAURENTS: Not quite that bad, but the reason he wanted me was because I was a playwright and he was going to film a play. Actually, I wrote a whole other screenplay or dialogue for all these characters to say in the background on the set. He wasn't much interested in anything on that picture. Again, he loved the whole kinky idea of it, but it was the camera that was the star. They had a great presentation for the press about how thoroughly this thing had been rehearsed. Jimmy Stewart, who was a very affable man and very quiet (drank a lot, too), said that the only thing that has been rehearsed around here is the camera. And it was perfectly true. As everybody knows, on a Hitchcock picture he saw everything on the screen without a viewfinder. He knew it all before the picture was shot. He was usually bored because it was all done in his mind. On *Rope* it was very difficult to coordinate the movements of the actors, who instead of being concerned with acting were more concerned with not tripping over cables and getting out of the way of the camera, which was all he was concerned with. It was very interesting, but weird.

SREBNICK: I would also ask Mr. Stefano and Mr. Hunter, since you both worked with source materials, what were the major issues in adaptation? I assume you were both asked to read the source material.

STEFANO: I was sent a copy of *Psycho* by Robert Bloch. As I read along, I was very fascinated with this young man and his mother and their continual arguing and her murderous hostility toward him. I thought it was very fascinating. Then, when I got to the end of the book, I found out that the mother had been dead and that Norman was his mother. It presented an incredible visual problem, because I didn't see how you could have him talking with his mother for the first twenty or thirty minutes and not show her. How long would an audience put up with that? I thought it was unfilmable until I was on my way to my first meeting with Hitchcock. I thought, ''What if this movie was about a young woman who's in a relationship that's not going anywhere because her boyfriend has all kinds of problems?'' By the time I got to the studio, I had worked out the first twenty minutes of the film, all about Marion Crane, up to that point when she gets murdered. I told my idea to Hitch who was quiet for a moment, then he leaned forward and said, ''We could get a star!'' I loved the idea because at that time nobody ever killed stars in the first twenty minutes of a movie. It was unheard of that this would happen.

I knew at that moment that I had the job because this was probably the problem he was wrestling with: how to get the audience involved in this character. I found out many years later that he had already had a script for *Psycho*. (You're never told this: according to the Writer's Guild you're supposed to be told, but nobody ever follows that rule and nobody ever reports them to the Writer's Guild if they don't follow the rule). The movie then became possible because there was no reason to directly see the mother. We think we see her during the murder. So for the rest of the movie, for me, the job was to keep the audience from wondering why we were not having any scenes with the mother. It was very important to me that you didn't know that she wasn't there. Other than that, we never discussed the book again. I kind of went at it as if it were an original screenplay, which the first thirty pages are. I thought that it worked that way and Hitch did too. Fortunately, he liked the idea. That's pretty much the story of the source material.

SREBNICK: Thank you. Mr. Hunter, what about Daphne du Maurier's novella?

HUNTER: Poor lady. As I said, it was thrown out. The only thing we kept from it was the finch attack down the chimney, because this happened in the novella. We used it to good effect in the film. Hitch once said to me, "Evan, there are only two stars in this film: the birds and me!"And then he hesitated and said, "And you of course." I was reminded of this when Joe was talking about Hitch saying "We could get a star." That's a stroke of genius. I remember when he came up with the advertising slogan for the film and he called in all the executives at Universal. They came into his office and he said, "This is what it's going to be: 'The birds is coming.' " One of the young Turks in the office said, "Excuse me, Mr. Hitchcock, sir, you mean 'The birds are coming,' don't you?"

What happened to the story? It was gone. I don't think Daphne du Maurier was too thrilled about that. I wouldn't have been happy. I've been on both ends of this. I've had my novels translated to the screen by other writers. I've done other people's novels for the screen or television. Whenever I'm doing it, I think of it as translating the book—just using the book and translating it to another medium, making it visual and not internal as most novels are. A lot of writers come to the task as if they must rewrite the whole book. I didn't try to do that when I was doing *Marnie*. With *The Birds* I had *carte blanche* to throw it away and come up with a whole new story.

SREBNICK: At this point, unless there are more comments from the writers, I would like to open up the discussion and invite questions from the audience.

QUESTION: I'm a fan and a psychologist, which is maybe why I'm a fan. I have two questions about *The Birds*. First, there was always a hint that maybe Melanie coming to that town is what caused the birds to attack. Even some of the townspeople say that. I'm wondering if that's really in there or I'm just seeing it. The second thing I want to know is your vision of what happens after *The Birds* ends.

HUNTER: That lingering suspicion that perhaps Melanie is causing all this was sort of a remnant of one of the ideas I had gone out to the coast with that we shot down and discarded. The thought was that Melanie would not be a sophisticated madcap heiress, but a schoolteacher coming to this little town of Bodega Bay who begins to teach. Suddenly bird attacks start. Because she is a stranger in town and the alien force in a sense, they begin blaming it on her. This probably lingered as an unconscious element in the final movie. Hitch added a scene to the Tides restaurant sequence where the mother of the two children accuses Melanie. He added a line there that I had not written about how she's the cause of all this before Melanie slaps her.

The other question, about the ending: there were ten pages of script that were not shot at the end of the film. They indicated a much wider attack of birds than just on this little town of Bodega Bay. There is some uncertainty as to whether the birds would be in San Francisco when they get there. I later thought of doing a sequel to *The Birds* where Tippi and Rod Taylor are married and their daughter is Tippi's real daughter, Melanie Griffith, and she's marrying Tom Cruise. They're back at the farmhouse for the wedding too. Veronica Cartwright is all grown up now and a very good actress, and she's there for the wedding. Birds attack again. Tom Cruise and Melanie Griffith flee the house and start cross-country. It's an apocalypse. The birds are taking over everywhere. It would have been a sort of a metaphor for nuclear warfare. But we never did it.

QUESTION: I have a question for Mr. Laurents about *Rope*. It was inspired by the Leopold-Loeb murders, which in turn were inspired by Friedrich Nietzsche's writings. There's an explicit reference to Nietzsche in the film, which seems very unusual, given that he was a very obscure philosopher in the nineteen-fifties in the United States, and not very popular. I just wondered if it was your decision to put that in. Did Hitchcock ever talk about Nietzsche's influence upon him?

LAURENTS: I put that in. I tried to lay in as much as I could about homosexuality without saying it, and about the whole superman theory. Actually, I didn't think that I'd get away with as much of it as I did. He didn't care. As Joe and Evan said, he wasn't interested in the words really. They may disagree, but I think he was just fascinated with the idea of a kinky murder. What I said about it was up to me. Does that satisfy you?

QUESTION (continued): I guess so. He never asked questions, didn't give you any input? He just let you run with it then?

LAURENTS: Oh yes. He gave me a free rein there.

QUESTION: I'm wondering if the three of you could say to what extent you were present on the set during the shooting. To what extent, if any, was there rewriting going on during shooting or even restructuring of scenes?

STEFANO: I was on the set almost every day for one reason. Hitch had seen a television spectacular, as they were called in those days, that I had done with Tony Curtis and wanted to know if we could do a two hour *Ford Startime* movie. He was fascinated by the idea of doing a movie-length piece for television. During the shooting of *Psycho*, we were talking about the possibilities of what this could be. I had hit upon a couple of thoughts. Whenever he finished a scene and said ''cut,'' he would come to where I was or he would go to his chair and I would go over to him. We would be discussing this. We rarely discussed *Psycho*. I think in both our minds the movie was finished.

When I finished the script, he said that he would like me to go to his house one morning and we'd just break it down into shots so that they could put it on the board. I had written mainly master scenes and we broke them down together. Then when we were finished, he asked Alma if they had any champagne in the house. She said they did, but that it was warm. He said that if I wouldn't tell anybody we'd put it over some ice cubes and toast this movie that was about to start the following week. He said that the fun part is over, which I thought was a little bit sad. At the same time it did, at that moment, turn into work for him because he had to get these people to do what he had seen in his mind. It is a little easier and more pleasant to do it if you're discussing how you're going to shoot a scene or what the people are going to say in it. He was always dressed the way he was described. That's the way he was on the set. He was very quiet. His set reminded me very much of a hospital waiting room. There was hardly any talk. Nobody ever said anything that they didn't have to say. It was very formal, but warm. It was nice. Nobody was in a bad mood. Everybody there seemed to be so perfectly happy to be working with Hitchcock.

One day, he asked me to look at the scene where Marion goes into the ladies room of the used car dealership to go through her papers. He said, ''Do you like the way this is set up?'' I was surprised because he didn't usually ask me questions like that. I said, ''No, I don't like it.'' It was very blank, and it looked like a TV set (which is what it was, incidentally). So he said, ''All right we'll take care of it.'' I went back out and a little bit later I saw the set and I saw the camera. I saw he had tilted it and put a mirror in the room so that when Janet is going through her bag we're seeing her in the mirror as well as her activity, showing the dual personality that had suddenly exploded. She had gone ''a little mad.''

It was interesting that he involved me in what he was doing, especially in the shower sequence. At the same time, he didn't seem to involve anybody else. He didn't involve the actors in what they were having to do. I think his attitude was that he and the writer created the movie and when their work was finished, the movie was finished. He rarely went far away from where he had been. This was maybe more true with *Psycho* than *The Birds* and other movies that cost a lot more. *Psycho*, in his mind, would cost less than a million dollars, preferably $800,000. He wanted to do it that way because a company called American International was making very inexpensive movies and making a lot of money on them. He said, "What if we did one?" So it was his notion that he would do one of these very low budget movies, but that it would be good. And he was right. It was a wonderful way to make a movie. I've since felt that life would be better if every movie could cost under a million dollars.

HUNTER: You were a tough act to follow, Joe. I think audiences who came to see *The Birds* were expecting the same kind of screams and thrills that they had gotten in *Psycho*. If I had to do it all over again, I would have started immediately with a bird attack. Frame one, boom, a bird hits somebody on the head.

STEFANO: Didn't a bird almost hit her in San Francisco?

HUNTER: No, they just look up at the sky and she smiles, "My, isn't it unusual all these birds up there? They sometimes get lost in the fog," or whatever the language was.

STEFANO: Well, maybe you should have started with her in a hotel room shacking up with her boyfriend.

HUNTER: Yes. Speaking of silence on the set, I rarely saw Hitch give any direction to anyone. Did you?

STEFANO: I didn't either.

HUNTER: He and Tippi had a code word: it was "Gorki." G-O-R-K-I, the writer. Her voice had a tendency to get strident sometimes because she wasn't a trained actress. He would just say "Gorki" very quietly, "Gorki," as he passed her by. She knew that when they did the next take she had to watch the level of her voice. But I rarely saw him giving direction to anyone.

STEFANO: I never saw an actor ask for direction.

LAURENTS: I saw a lot of it.

STEFANO: You did?

LAURENTS: I obviously had a very different experience. I was on the set every day. There weren't many days because it was all shot on one set. Incidentally, about his manner of dress, I spent several weekends at his country house in the mountains north of San Francisco, and he wore that same black suit, black tie, and white shirt, and so forth. But on the set there was one interesting thing.

STEFANO: He had only one suit, Arthur.

HUNTER: No, he had eighty of the same suit.

LAURENTS: Yes, probably. Anyway, there was one interesting thing, not about him, but about the character of the maid in *Rope*. Most of the time on the set everybody sat around while, as Jimmy Stewart said, "the camera was rehearsed." But the other actors made the maid sit apart from them. They treated her like a maid. Anyway, he would direct each one of them. It was a combination of what he wanted from them and what he wanted them to do for the camera. He would say, "And you smile here and it goes!" That was acting! What I had to do was write background dialogue for this party that was going on all the time. I must say I had a lot of fun with it. I thought it was much funnier than anything said on the screen. It's a pity you can't hear a lot of it.

HUNTER: I was on the set by accident when they were shooting *The Birds* because I was working on *Marnie* and we were having discussions. You asked about what kind of rewriting was done. A lot of rewriting was being done, but not by me. Rod Taylor came over one day and said, "Did you write this scene?" And I read it and I said, "No, I didn't." And he said," Well, we're shooting it today." So I went over to Hitch and said, "Hitch, I just read this scene and I really think it has no place in the movie. I really think it's badly written." It's the scene at the birthday party before the birds attack the children. Tippi and Mitch go up on a dune with martini glasses and drink martinis. She begins telling him about her awful childhood when her mother ran off with quote, "a hotel man from the east" unquote. I said, "it doesn't sound like her; it doesn't even sound American. I really don't think you should shoot this Hitch." He looked at me and said, "Are you going to trust me or a two-bit actor?" They shot it and it is in the movie. I think Hitch wrote the scene himself. I strongly suspect it.

STEFANO: I'd like to tell you about something that happened on the first day of shooting. Hitchcock came over to me and said, "Mr. Gavin would like to make a change in your script." He said, "Maybe you'd better talk to him." So I said, "Is this anything serious that I need to really pay a lot of attention to?" And he said, "Well, it's up to you." So I went over to John Gavin and said, "What's our problem here?" He said, "Everything's fine, except must I appear naked from the waist up?" I said, "Well, you know, you've just had sex with this woman and you're coming out of the bathroom and the only reason you have your pants on is because otherwise we would not have gotten a go on this." And he said, "Well, I just don't like to be without a shirt." I said, "That's what the scene calls for," and I never heard another word about it. He appeared, as you know, without a shirt. Hitch never said a word about it. He apparently did not go back to Hitchcock to see if I was crazy, or if I could be thrown off the set, or something. It was an interesting thing because Hitch changed things visually, but he never changed the dialogue. The only thing he did was cut some stuff when it got near the final cut.

QUESTION: I have a question for Mr. Stefano and Mr. Hunter. There are two beautifully choreographed scenes that you wrote: the shower scene and the jungle gym scene outside the school with the birds coming in—the juxtaposition between the songs the children are singing and her nervous cigarette smoking. I'm curious. How much was this detailed out in your original scripts? How choreographed was it in its original form?

HUNTER: I wrote all the shots for the jungle gym sequence. In fact, I also got the song from my children, who were in elementary school at the time. This was a song they used to sing, that they were taught in whatever grade they were in. I got a call from the coast saying that we needed some more lyrics. I'm a member of ASCAP now because of this. So I wrote another whole twelve sets of lyrics so that the birds could keep gathering on the jungle gym. So that was all really choreographed in the script. What was not choreographed in the script and what is one of the most brilliant scenes in the movie is when Tippi Hedren is trapped in the telephone booth and the birds are smashing into it and the man comes by with blood streaming down his face. This was all Hitch's invention, and it was marvelous, I thought.

STEFANO: We discussed the shower scene and Saul Bass did a storyboard on it. Hitch told me I was not to put it in the screenplay. He didn't want anybody to know what this scene was going to look like. There was a tremendous air of secrecy on the set. Nobody ever talked about it outside the sound stage. If you went to lunch, you did not discuss what was being done. It was an incredibly secret affair. He felt that scripts, somehow, always managed to get out. Everybody in all the studios always has a copy of the script that you just started shooting. Nobody ever knows how they get it, but they get it. He said, "Indicate that she's going to get murdered, but spread it out and make it longer. Say whatever you want to say, but don't say anything to indicate that this is going to be a very brief, very violent scene." That was it.

LAURENTS: You guys seem to have been much more fortunate than I was. You guys both seem to have been very involved in the making of the movie. I was not. Just on a few occasions and again, as I said, just by accident.

STEFANO: That's more typical actually that the writer is not involved in film making.

QUESTION: Two brief questions, one for Mr. Stefano, the other for Mr. Hunter. Mr. Stefano, you also mentioned that you were involved in the remake of *Psycho*. I will not enter into that topic now. It just interests me. One horrible point in the remake, and one I consider almost a stroke of genius. Did you have anything to do with them? The horrible point is Norman observing Marion through the peephole while masturbating. It's not out of moralistic reasons that I think this is wrong, but, to put it in vulgar terms, if he were able to satisfactorily masturbate there would be no cause for him to slaughter her. What was your relation to that? The stroke of genius, I think, and the only one in the film is at the very end, the long final credits in the style of the nineties with a guitar improvising and a long crane shot withdrawing from the scene. That, I think, gives the specific flavor of the nineties. Did you have anything to do with these two features?

STEFANO: I was involved in Gus Van Sant's remake in that he called me and told me what he was planning to do and that he would like to talk with me. We had lunch, and I asked a question that many people later asked, which was "Why?" He said, "Well, you know if *Psycho* had been a play, your play would have been done 2000 times by now in different places." I thought, "Yes, that's an attractive idea, and it is nice to write a play and have people do it all over the world and see all these different interpretations of it." I somehow envisioned that Gus Van Sant was going to direct this movie. I had not envisioned Gus Van Sant subserviently copying every single thing in the original. I found out rather quickly that he really was not interested in any rewrites I had in mind. I felt that there were things that needed to be changed slightly.

I thought my best suggestion to Gus Van Sant was not to have the psychiatrist come in and tell these people on the set what he had just heard from Norman Bates as his mother in the cell. Instead, my idea was to have the psychiatrist go into the place where Norman was and have him talk with Norman, who has totally become his mother. The "mother," then, would be telling the audience what they need to know. Gus liked that idea very much, but he said that it was a shame we didn't do it that way the first time. I said, "Well, you know, isn't that what this is about? Aren't we going to fix some things here?" It finally wound up that he agreed to change just one thing: that the amount of money to buy the house should be different. Marion would steal $400,000 instead of $40,000. I told him, "First of all, this man whose money it is that she steals talks about buying his child a house for a wedding present and I don't know where he's going to find one for $40,000." So, we made it $400,000. Then he changed some motel prices, very practical things. But he wouldn't give the detective a cell phone. The detective still had to use a public phone booth somewhere. Early on, I realized that we weren't going to see much of Mr. Van Sant in the new version. We were going to see almost a replica, except it was going to be in color.

When I was on the set, I also saw that suddenly actors were now involved in changing their characters. Anne Heche had no desire at all to play the character as written, but she still had to say the same dialogue. So, a different person was saying Marion's dialogue. It was so jarring. I offered to rewrite the scene so she could play it with the character that she wanted to play. I began to get very tired of the project because it seemed to me that the actors were just doing whatever they felt like, and that if Gus was going to do it shot for shot and line for line, then let's see it done correctly. Let's do that then. But you have to play the same characters; otherwise I'd have wanted to change the dialogue. It was strange. In post-production he added some things that were not in the original movie. It was a very strange experiment. I felt that it had gone terribly awry.

LAURENTS: I thought the picture worked best the same place the original worked best, until Norman Bates arrives. I think Tony Perkins is so stamped on that part that you could not possibly make another picture. They made a musical of *Big*, but they didn't have Tom Hanks and they should have stayed home. When a personality gets so identified with a role, I think you're dead, and I think that's what happened there.

STEFANO: And Tony played it twice again, so it was really indelible.

LAURENTS: Yes.

QUESTION (continued): Mr. Hunter, you said everything was to be erased from the novella by Daphne du Maurier. I like to make mental experiments. One of my favorites is to imagine *The Birds* without the birds. I think it functions. We get, I admit, a slightly boring melodrama of the fifties with the son and the oppressive mother and so on. The first quarter of an hour is screwball comedy. It then develops into a kind of Tennessee Williams drama. So, it stands on its own. I'm not saying it's very good drama, but I can imagine *The Birds* without the birds. But, unfortunately, there are birds. It's easy for you to say we didn't disclose the meaning, but you must have an idea. I know this is an intrusive, politically incorrect question. But why do the birds attack? You must have a theory.

STEFANO: My answer to the question as to why the birds did it? Because Alfred Hitchcock told them to.

HUNTER: I always thought that the whole story in *The Birds* was marking time between attacks. I always felt that way, anyway. We were constructing some kind of story that nobody was interested in at all. We just wanted to see birds hitting people. I did, anyway.

QUESTION: This is a question for all the members of the panel. You spoke of Hitchcock's interest in your psychoanalytic sessions . . .

LAURENTS: I didn't.

QUESTION (continued): Did you have discussions with him where he talked about his films in psychological terms?

STEFANO: I didn't. As I said, he was not really that interested in why the characters were doing what they were doing. He was not really interested in that. He liked to think that he was above what Arthur calls "kink." No one ever said to him that this is rather kinky business here, which was strange, because I think that off the set Mr. Hitchcock also liked kinky things and he liked kinky stories. A lot of our time together was spent gossiping about the kinkiness of the people we all knew. It was great fun for him, but he never acted as though he were putting it on screen.

LAURENTS: I never heard him talk about anything psychological—a lot about kink. His main concern was about what he called the "icebox trade." That was, he said, when "they get home from the picture and he takes a beer from the icebox and she takes a soda and one of them says 'Why didn't they call the police?' " Curiously enough, if you see *Strangers on a Train*, why didn't they call the police?

HUNTER: We never had any psychological discussions about *The Birds*, but when I was working on *Marnie* he asked me to write a letter to Tippi explaining the character's psychology. She was a strange character who committed robberies and was frigid and had witnessed a murder in her youth. He asked me to write a letter explaining her psychology after

Tippi had gotten the part. But when the thought of who was going to play Marnie first came up, I asked him who he had in mind. As if we were being eavesdropped upon, he mouthed the word "Grace."

QUESTION: What do you think will be the lasting appeal of Hitchcock films for audiences in the next century, and do you think that Hitchcock has a status he deserves or do you think it's been overblown?

LAURENTS: With the risk of getting stones thrown at me, I think movies are overanalyzed. I mean this business about *The Birds*. It was obviously made for the birds! Why make a big deal about it? That's what it's about. It's clearly there, and either you went for it or you didn't. I did a picture once called *Caught*, and it ran out of money. We had to shoot twelve days in four and I had to rewrite it. It was directed by a man named Max Ophuls. To save money everything had black velours and a lot of mist. Pauline Kael, who is the dean of the whole tribe of film critics, commented on the scenic murkiness, which commented on the psychological murkiness. Well, it was money! There wasn't enough money, so we had murky sets! It's that simple. So far as Hitchcock, I don't know, and I frankly think what does it matter? The man's gone and he's not going to enjoy it or know one way or the other.

HUNTER: I think that's the irony of it—a man who when I was working with him was so concerned with recognition and gaining respectability—that we are sitting here together thirty-seven years later, or whatever it is, and paying great homage to him. I think this would have pleased him enormously if he were still alive.

STEFANO: I think the sadness of Hitchcock's hundredth birthday is that he didn't live to see it. I don't think anybody would have enjoyed the fuss that's been made this year more than he would. He would say, of course, that he didn't enjoy it. He would pass it off and change the subject, but there would be a look in his face and in his eyes that would say it's about time.

LAURENTS: You have to remember that this is a man who found a way to put himself into every one of his pictures, which says something about ego.

QUESTION: I have two questions for Mr. Hunter. I'm fascinated with the idea that *The Birds* began as a screwball comedy. The other questioner's words are ringing in my ears: "a boring Tennessee Williams melodrama." I didn't find it boring by any means. But this austere melodrama that it winds up being for the most part, I just can't imagine the road from screwball comedy to that. I'm curious about how this took place. For Mr. Stefano, did you and Hitchcock ever discuss the influence of the French picture *Diabolique* on *Psycho*? Did that ever figure in any of your conversations together?

HUNTER: Screwball comedy. When I first proposed the idea, he liked it, and in our minds we were thinking of Cary Grant and Grace Kelly, although we knew we weren't going to get them. (We were not going to get Cary Grant because Hitch said, "I'm not going to give him fifty percent of the movie!"And Grace Kelly we were not going to get because "She's off in Monaco being a princess, isn't she?") But these were the characters in our heads when I was writing *The Birds* and when we were discussing it. We did not get them, and I think it suffered somewhat. I felt the chemistry was totally lacking between Rod Taylor and Tippi Hedren. I think they were missing the point, and I think Hitch may have missed the point along the way too. I think he had grave misgivings about the script as the movie was being shot. I think, more and more, he began to lose confidence in my script and began to turn it in different directions which may have resulted in Tennessee Williams. I still think it's a good idea. I still thinks it's a lovely idea that suddenly somebody gets hit on the head in the midst of what we think is going to be a boy-girl love story. What I did not realize was that I really had the burden of *Psycho*. I was not joking when I said that it was a tough act to follow. I think the audience was sitting there and getting itchy about when the birds are coming. When are they coming? Why are we listening to all this silly nonsense between these two people? Where are the birds? That was a grave error, perhaps.

STEFANO: In regard to *Diabolique*. At one point toward the end of our work on the script, Hitchcock asked me if I thought there was anything that might be compared to *Diabolique* in any way or related to it in any way. I didn't think so and he didn't think so either, but he felt that maybe we'd better look at it. So we went into a screening room and watched *Diabolique*. There wasn't really anything similar in what we were talking about and that movie. My recollection is that Hitch shrugged it off. Maybe somebody had said something to him about *Diabolique*, but he wasn't terribly impressed with it.

QUESTION: I just wanted to comment to Mr. Laurents: not to worry. We're really used to being accused of over-analysis. I wrote a book on Ophuls which is very over-analytical. My questions are little, nagging, detail questions. As we watch these films again and again, especially with our students, they say, ''But they didn't intend that. That detail doesn't mean anything.'' We, of course, argue with them. One of the details, Mr. Stefano, that bothers me every time I see the film is in the scene you were discussing where Marion is selling her car. Was there discussion of the license tags of the cars—that ANL was chosen as one of the license tags?

STEFANO: I have no idea. I don't even remember what it says. The interesting thing to me is that at the time you're making this movie you have absolutely no idea that people might be seeing it a year hence—we're talking about 1960—let alone forty years later, or that people would ever be analyzing the movie so closely. Everybody does what they like in making a movie and what they think is good. Somebody gets the job of going out and getting the cars that we need. In the used car lot, cars would have license plates on them. The only thing we were concerned about with regard to the plates was the change from Arizona to California. It was very important that you understand that she was now in California. And I'll tell you why that was important, and that is because we have told you she only sees her boyfriend when he flies in on business. I felt that if we changed the state that it would make more sense. Certainly in 1959 it made more sense that he flew in from another state than from somewhere in California. I wanted it to start out in Arizona and end up in California.

QUESTION (continued): Okay. I have just another couple of detail questions. First, in writing the screenplay for *Psycho*, do you remember reading another work by Robert Bloch, a story called "The Real Bad Friend," which is also about a male character with a multiple personality? There have been claims that it was another source.

STEFANO: No, I never read that.

QUESTION (continued): My final question: in the novel of *Psycho*, Marion is decapitated in the shower. Who decided not to decapitate her in the film?

STEFANO: I decided that I didn't want to see this woman in the shower getting killed and having her head cut off. Hitchcock agreed that it would be nothing he would want to put on film.

QUESTION (continued): One final, small question about *The Birds* for Mr. Hunter. Do you remember whose idea it was for Mitch's mom to go out in the truck and find the guy with his eyes gouged out? Because we're all very fascinated by moms in Hitchcock.

HUNTER: Yes, it was mine. The long journey home was to cover a love scene between Mitch and Melanie outside. In a scene that was cut, Melanie looks at Mitch from the window. We see him doing something outside, and what he's doing is raking up dead birds. We couldn't come close in on it because of the animal rights people. She then comes out and they try to work out together why this is happening. There's a comic scene where they conjure up a bird revolutionary in the hills getting all the birds together to rise and attack: "We have nothing to lose but our feathers," that kind of thing. They end up frightening themselves, or at least frightening her. He grabs her and they're kissing when the truck appears. If you recall, we see them breaking apart through the windshield of the truck, although we never saw them getting together. Throughout the rest of the film, she's calling him "darling" and we have no idea why. We never have seen them kiss or embrace or anything, and now she's calling him darling and we go, "Huh?" After that long drive out, mother comes back and we then cut away to the two of them while she comes into the driveway, still at top speed.

QUESTION: I have a question for all three gentlemen. You've all spoken about the story conferences that you would have with Hitchcock before you wrote the screenplay, apparently usually over lunch. Since we're all wondering how much of a contribution he made to the screenplay, not necessarily the dialogue but the story and the characters, could you all give us an estimate as to how much of the screenplay came from him in terms of plot and character and how much was from you?

STEFANO: You mean as a percentage, so to speak?

QUESTION (continued): Just roughly.

STEFANO: If this were being negotiated with the Writers Guild, I would say that his contribution to the screenplay consisted mainly of stopping me if he thought something should be other than what I was talking about. I described the action as it would happen, what the people would be saying, what they'd be talking about, and if he thought something might present a problem, he would then speak about that. I don't ever remember him saying that we should do this, or this is how a scene should work. He just behaved as if it was not his job to do that. He spoke to me once about an actor who had given a very disappointing performance in one of his movies, that he was mainly disappointed because his feeling was that when you got to be in one of his movies, you ought to know what you were doing. An actor who was up there not knowing what he or she was doing was disturbing to him. To him it was like, "How did he get this far?" I think he felt that way about scripts too, that you knew what you were doing by the time you were working on a movie with him. It was, at once, a compliment and a way of shutting you up about trying to get him to give you too much information.

HUNTER: I agree. As I said earlier, his role seemed to be more editorial than it was creative in terms of writing the script. I still suspect he wrote that scene on the dunes, but that's one tenth of one percent, perhaps less. I have no proof that he did write it.

LAURENTS: The only thing he asked me was whether the dialogue could cover some visual idea he had, and if it couldn't, could I adjust it. His role was minor, practically non-existent. So far as casting, he was curiously either perverse or contradictory. He wanted an American version of the English stage play and he cast two English actors, Cedric Hardwicke and Constance Collier. He was very worried about Constance. He said, "Her voice is so low. Will people think she's a lesbian?"

QUESTION: I'm particularly interested in Hitchcock's television work. This question is for Mr. Stefano and, to some extent, Mr. Hunter as well. You worked with Hitchcock on both his television work as well as film. I was wondering if Hitchcock ever said anything to you about his thoughts generally on television but also on creating television himself and perhaps if he expressed any views on any television programs that you made yourselves?

STEFANO: I never worked on television with him, nor did I ever hear him say anything about any situation or story being right for television or wrong for films or vice versa. I don't think he had any sense of it being any different.

HUNTER: He had adapted two short stories I had written for his half-hour show, one called "Vicious Circle" and the other called "First Defense." I also adapted a short story by a man named Robert Turner called "Appointment at Eleven." I adapted that for his half-hour show. He never commented to me on any of them. I always suspected that he hired me for *The Birds* because of my adaptation of that story. I asked him one time, "Why did you hire me?" And he said, "I make it my business to know what's going on Evan," which was very mysterious. I think it was because of "Appointment at Eleven," which took place entirely in the kid's head, which I had to open up, as they say. Since the du Maurier novella took place in a cottage with just an inarticulate farmer and his wife, I think he hired me to open it up, so to speak. We never discussed television or his role in television. We just discussed *The Birds* and later *Marnie*. That was it.

QUESTION (continued): I guess I'll just have to keep searching for quotes on television and Hitchcock. The only one I have at the moment is from Mr. Norman Lloyd, a biographical book in which he said to Mr. Lloyd that in television you just get up close. That's the only thing he said to Norman Lloyd about television aesthetics.

QUESTION: I have two questions for Mr. Stefano. First, you said you only had one or two credits before *Psycho*. I was just wondering how you got the responsibility for an Alfred

Hitchcock picture. The other concerns all the underlying humor in *Psycho*. I haven't read the book so I don't know if it is in the original book, or if it is part of your screenplay, or any influence by Hitchcock?

STEFANO: The humor, as I recall, was not in the book. The characters were very different in the book. Norman was a much older man. He was in his forties, and he was a drunk—nothing like the Norman Bates that you know. I find it hard not to put some humor in things because it just seems to happen when I'm writing. I don't intend to do it very often. I was aware that I was dealing here with a director who was a very witty man and said some very funny things and had some very funny sensibilities. He never said anything that was a big joke, for instance, but he looked at things in a humorous way. I have read that he claimed that *Psycho* was a comedy. I always thought that it was a charming notion on his part, just the way he said that actors should be treated like cattle. He said things that were rather outrageous but perhaps came to him at that moment to say them. I think that he liked the fact that there was humor. The only humorous line that he ever commented on to me was after the murder of Marion, when we go to Sam's hardware store and her sister comes in. I had a woman buying some insecticide, and she's reading the label. She says something like "They tell you how it kills them, but they don't tell you whether it's painless." He thought that was a marvelous line. If you see the movie again, you'll notice that it gets quiet right at that moment so that the line can be heard. I thought it would probably be lost in the action otherwise. He really liked it.

QUESTION (continued): How did you get the assignment to write *Psycho*?

STEFANO: I had done one movie and one television show, and I felt people in the business were acting like I knew everything that I needed to know and were depending on me. I thought that this wasn't going to work, so I went to someone I knew at MCA, which was then the biggest agency, and I told them that I would like to be with their agency. I gave them a list of ten directors I wanted to work with, any one of whom I felt could teach me how to make movies. Hitchcock was on that list. I later found out that they had worked very hard to get him to meet me. He hadn't liked the movie I had written, *The Black Orchid*. He also thought I was kind of a street kid from south Philadelphia (he was right) and that I probably didn't have the sophistication that he was used to. I guess someone from MCA suggested that maybe that was exactly what he ought to have. So he agreed to meet me. As I think I have already said, the first thing I told him was how I would make the picture. I think he kind of liked that.

QUESTION: One final question. Back to the screwball comedy business. The beginning of *The Birds* always struck me as more of a Doris Day/Rock Hudson kind of thing. It is so prolonged that it must have been part of your intention. You now say that you regret it. I'm wondering, since the whole film seems to me like a satire in a way of that kind of film, whether Hitchcock ever spoke about other films and other directors, and what he said?

HUNTER: I'm trying to remember. I don't recall him ever talking about any other directors. Well, he talked about Truffaut, because at the time I think they were setting up the interviews with Truffaut. While I was working on *Marnie*, certainly, they were setting up the Truffaut interviews. So he spoke about him. He spoke about actors a lot—actors he had worked with and actors he knew—but I think he was sort of egotistical. He thought he was "the director." I don't recall him ever discussing other directors or other films.

STEFANO: Can I tell you something about other directors? I once asked Hitchcock about the new up and coming directors, many of whom were coming to film from television in 1960.

I asked him if he had seen any of their stuff and he said that he had. I then asked him who he liked. He said, ''Well, I can't really judge them as directors,'' but then he named a director and said that he had been invited to a dinner party at this director's house. (I'm not going to tell you his name, so don't even ask me). He said that during the dinner the waiter served wine with a cloth around it, and it was not even cold wine. So why did he have that napkin wrapped around the bottle? I had the feeling that Hitchcock dismissed this man and his work forever. That mistake would be enough to judge his life's work.

SREBNICK: I hope you'll join me in thanking our screenwriters, not only for sharing their ideas with us but for their wonderful part in the creation of these films.

THE LODGER AND THE
ORIGINS OF HITCHCOCK'S AESTHETIC

RICHARD ALLEN

This paper has a dual focus: I seek to explore some of the origins of Hitchcock's aesthetic in late Victorian and early twentieth-century culture that lay the basis for what Hitchcock himself called the first Hitchcock film, *The Lodger* (1926). At the same time, I shall examine *The Lodger* itself as a work that lies at the origin of Hitchcock's aesthetic, for distilled in *The Lodger*, in highly condensed fashion, are artistic preoccupations that will last a lifetime.[1]

Hitchcock and the Legacy of Victorianism

Alfred Hitchcock was born in 1899 and raised in the London suburb of Leytonstone, located five miles east of the city center. Eleven years before, in 1888, in the areas of London's East End districts of Whitechapel and Spitalfields a few miles away from where Hitchcock grew up, a series of five singularly brutal murders occurred that were united by certain common characteristics. All the murdered women were known to be prostitutes and in each case their bodies had been ripped open and their internal organs removed; the murderer came to be known as Jack the Ripper. Four out of five of the murders took place in public spaces that, after the first murder, were heavily patrolled by policeman. Thus authorities concluded that the murderer must have had expertise in killing or in cutting up bodies, or at least in wielding a knife, since the execution and evisceration must have been swift to avoid detection. Since Whitechapel was a center for slaughtering cattle, the police focused their initial investigation upon the transient population of men who manned the cattle boats. Popular suspicion, fueled by the flames of anti-Semitism directed at the newly arrived population of eastern European Jews that were fanned by the sensationalist press, centered upon an innocent slippermaker, one John Pizer, dubbed Leather Apron, who was pursued by a raging mob through the streets and gave himself up to the police to escape their fury. However, the dominant theory came to be that the murders were the work of a doctor or a medical student and hence a man of the upper classes. The murderer was never caught. This fact, together with the obscenity of the crime, fuelled a vast popular discourse upon Jack the Ripper that was sustained for many, many years after the event, a discourse of which *The Lodger* forms a part.

The idea of the upper-class male sexual predation on women of the lower classes had already attained mythical proportions in the late Victorian imagination. In 1885, W.T Stead, editor of the *Pall Mall Gazette*, had written a series of exposés entitled "The Maiden Tribute of Modern Babylon," describing how poor "daughters of the people" were "snared, trapped, and outraged, either when under the influence of drugs or after a prolonged struggle in a locked room." They were "served up" nightly "as dainty morsels to minister to the passions of the rich," victims of a predatory Minator.[2] Stead was subsequently tried, convicted, and imprisoned for three months for engaging in the very procurement of young ladies that he described, but as a result of his exposé the Criminal Law Amendment Act of 1885 was passed, which raised the age of consent for young women from thirteen to sixteen, widened police power to prosecute prostitutes and brothel-keepers, and made "indecent acts" between consulting male adults illegal (the sexual procurement of men by men was a suppressed subtext of Stead's campaign). When the Ripper case burst into the headlines, Stead promoted the theory of an aristocratic predator and, according to Judith Walkowitz, he was the first to draw attention to the sexual origins of the crime and to invoke Stevenson's *Dr. Jekyll and Mr. Hyde*, published two years before, in explanation of the psychology of the murderer.[3] Stead's amateur psychological profile was given an official imprimatur by forensic expert Dr. Thomas Bond, who, in addition to citing *Dr. Jekyll and Mr. Hyde*, invoked

Krafft-Ebings' newly-minted theories of sexual perversion to profile the mind of a sexual sadist. Krafft-Ebing in turn included the Ripper in the next edition of *Psychopathia Sexualis* as a clinical specimen of "lust murder." The idea of Jack the Ripper as a gentleman by day and a murderous sexual predator/pervert by night defined the myth of the Ripper in ensuing years.

Framed by the Stevenson's trope of Jekyll and Hyde, the new discourse of psychopathology, and the "Maiden Tribute" scandals, the Jack the Ripper myth condensed anew Victorian anxieties about class and gender within the figure of the gentleman. Stevenson's Jekyll/Hyde is a gentleman bachelor scientist by day and a murderous troglodyte by night. There is no sense overtly conveyed in the novel that the "disreputable," "callous," and "violent" activities of Mr. Hyde, who drank "pleasure with bestial avidity from any degree of torture" are of an erotic kind. It is as if, as Walkowitz suggests, the two sides of Stevenson's character embody the two sides of Victorian London as seen through the lens of Lombrosian theories of criminal types, where the nature of the criminal mind is revealed through characteristic features of bodily posture and physiognomy. The Victorian gentleman fears an atavistic regression to the primitive lumpen-proletarian condition of the slum dweller. However, once the Jekyll/Hyde myth was deployed to explain the psychology of the Ripper, sexual anxieties supervened upon class anxieties. Hyde/Ripper was a murderous sexual predator whose bestial proclivities remained hidden beneath a veneer of gentleman-liness, that is, a veneer of both gentleness and propriety. The deeds of Jack the Ripper gave an existence or reality to the unspeakable actions of Dr. Jekyll that couldn't be narrated or told; the deformed and hideous body of Dr. Hyde pictured the true nature of the beast concealed beneath the gentle-manly exterior. The West End stage play adaptation of *Dr. Jekyll and Mr. Hyde* that opened in August 1888 starring Richard Mansfield adhered to Stead's interpretation of Jekyll/Hyde as a sex criminal whose sexual drive finds expression in violence toward the opposite sex.[4]

The Ripper's victims were prostitutes of the lower classes and the Jekyll/Ripper myth replays the stereotype of the prostitute-whore as a fallen woman. The idea of the fallen woman in the mid-Victorian imagination was not simply a moral category that defined a fall from goodness, but described a condition in which moral consciousness itself had been lost.[5] The fallen woman was someone who had lost her capacity to discriminate between right and wrong, who had abandoned her freedom or autonomy, and was therefore someone whose behavior was wholly governed by the forces of nature. The fallen woman had lost the capacity for authentic self-consciousness, self-determination, or self-control; she was an abject human being. The self-display of the prostitute manifested an inauthentic expression of self, a masquerade of identity; for once fallen, the fallen woman has lost the capacity for authentic self-determination. Of course, according to the ideology of the time, all women were incipiently fallen, defined against the masculine ideal of autonomy, self control, and the realization of self in action. In one sense the Jekyll/Ripper myth rehearsed a gendered idea of fallenness in the idea of the aristocratic Minator who preys at will upon fallen women, yet at the same time, it destabilized the gender polarities that defined the myth. Jekyll/Ripper is contaminated by his association with fallen women. Jekyll/Ripper at once manifests the same compulsive, determined behavior of the fallen women, and masquerades a false identity that disguises his true, bestial nature.

In 1891, three years after the London stage production of *Dr. Jekyll and Mr. Hyde,* and after he had moved from Oxford to live in London, Oscar Wilde published *The Picture of Dorian Gray.* In *Dorian Gray,* Wilde self-consciously dramatizes the relationship between the gentlemanly exterior and the bestial inner life that defines the character of Jekyll/Ripper by transposing the Jekyll/Ripper myth into the sensibility of *fin-de-siècle* decadence and aestheticism. The persona of the gentleman dandy is embodied in three characters: an earnest gentleman-artist, Basil Hallward; a decadent, idle aristocrat, Lord Henry Wotton; and Dorian

Gray, a young aesthete and idealist. Dorian Gray is afforded eternal youth by assuming the identity bequeathed upon him in an idealized portrait painted by Basil Hallward. Under the influence of the dandy, Lord Henry, this immunity to physical decay allows him to freely indulge his desires. However, the portrait unflinchingly registers his increasing depravity, just as Hyde reveals the inner soul of Jekyll.

The Picture of Dorian Gray is important to the development of the myth of Jekyll/Ripper and to Hitchcock's life-long preoccupation with that myth in at least four respects.

First, in Wilde the Jekyll/Ripper myth is self-consciously and playfully transposed into the realm of art. Wilde creates an analogy between the gentlemanly persona and the work of art in which the idea of the gentlemanly persona becomes an artful fabrication, a narcissistic idealization of the self, that harbors within its brilliant surface a core of dark, bestial desire. The decay of the idealized surface of the artwork renders literal in a visual pun the manner in which surface idealization masks a core of "corruption" and thereby suggests the very thing that it seems so thoroughly to conceal.

Second, the decaying portrait of the idealized image self consciously puns upon the idea that art, considered as a form of idealization which defies the temporality of human mortality and decay, kills what it represents. Art replaces life for the aesthete. Wilde celebrates the converse, murder as a form of art, in his essay "Pencil, Pen, and Poison," whose subject is the artist/murderer Thomas Wainwright and whose title, as Peter Conrad points out, playfully alliterates upon the connection between art and murder.[6]

Third, in *Dorian Gray*, art not only defies the temporality of human mortality and decay but also implicitly defies the facile optimism, the sense of futurity, of the romance narrative, with its logic of character development and anticipation of a happy ending. The creation of the artwork involves a displaced expression of perversion that "suspends" the logic of narrative development. In the brief romance between Dorian and the lower-class "actress" Sybil, Sybil's "performance" of the lover, her self-conscious masquerade of femininity, mirrors the gentlemanly masquerade of the dandy Dorian. The moment that Sybil resolves to step outside her roles as a lover, assume her real-life identity as a woman, and "fall" in love with Dorian, Dorian's desire is quenched and Sybil, rejected, precipitously dies by her own hand.

Fourth, *The Picture of Dorian Gray* seems to entertain the possibility of homosexual desire in the triangular relationship between its male protagonists, only to deny it, as if the possibility of that desire can be articulated only through aestheticization, in particular the aestheticization of the male body, that is linked to deadliness and perversion, to the destruction of romance and the promise of the happy end. Of course, the link intimated by the novel between homosexual perversion and aestheticism can be homophobically conceived. Indeed, Wilde's book was cited as "evidence" for Wilde's degeneracy in his trial. Yet, by the same token, Wilde's aestheticism triumphantly subverts the value system of Victorian society to which it nonetheless subscribes.

Shortly after the publication of *The Picture of Dorian Gray*, the nature of "perversion" and its relationship to the making of art began to be theorized by Freud. In Freud's explicit theory of creativity—the theory of sublimation—perversion and sublimation are contrasting outcomes of the sexual instinct in human development. "Perversions," Freud writes, "are the development of germs, all of which are contained in the undifferentiated sexual dispositions of the child, and which, by being suppressed or being diverted to higher, asexual aims—by being sublimated—are destined to provide the energy for a great number of our cultural achievements."[7] However, as Freudian theorist Janine Chasseguet-Smirgel has argued, Freud's concept of idealization intimates a different account of the relation of perversion to creativity in which the sexual instinct is directly implicated in aesthetic activity, where aesthetic activity is not a displacement of perversion but an enactment or realization of it.[8] Freud suggests in his essay "On Narcissism" that "idealization" involves not a deflection of sexual instinct from sexual satisfaction but an investment of the sexual instinct in the aggrandization of self in an objectified "idealized" form that seems very like the body of the dandy as it is conceived by Wilde.[9]

The "pervert's" self-objectification is motivated by an impulse to sustain the illusion that "polymorphous" sexual impulses, which appear debased or abject in relationship to socially sanctioned forms of normative masculinity, are in fact equal to—indeed better than—the normative expression of masculinity embodied in the Victorian father. The incipient "pervert" idealizes his abject, fragmented, infantile state with respect to heterosexual genital sexuality, as if it is whole and perfect, as if it were adequate too or even better than the phallic sexuality of the father, adequate in particular, to meeting the needs of the mother. However the illusion of the narcissist is a fragile one: the surface of the narcissistic body is one whose idealized perfection intimates an abject core that lies beneath. For Freud, narcissistic illusion is sustained by fetishistic props other than the body of the self. These props often have the qualities at once of something unbroken and smooth and yet also something whose surface appearance conceals dirtiness, like a patent leather shoe. The fetish is an object that through the idealization of surface at once reveals and conceals a core of abjection.

In the context of Freudian theory, the link between the body of the aesthete and the artwork in aestheticism becomes apparent. The artwork, considered as a fetish object that involves the fabrication of perfect, more than real, surfaces that at once conceal and reveal an abject core is an extension of the body of the dandy-aesthete. It is the artwork conceived in this way as a fetish extension of the narcissistic body that is joked upon in Wilde's parable of Dorian Gray, where the idealized surface of the painting takes the form of a corrupted body, while the corrupted body of the dandy takes on the form of an idealized surface. Equally, it seems to me that as a medium of "idealization," as a medium of surface, film appealed to Hitchcock with a self-consciousness that equals that of Wilde. As a medium of surfaces that precluded the kind of depth characterization afforded by the novel or even dramatic dialogue, silent cinema was used by Hitchcock to convey the sense that conventional forms of plotting and characterization embodied in the romance narrative were at once idealized surface, a hyperbolic reality more real than reality itself, and yet only skin deep. The performance of gentlemanliness and the masquerade of femininity, the romantic pursuit that is dramatized in self-consciously oedipal plots and realized in the supremely explosive moment of the kiss: all this in Hitchcock's work, however elaborated and fully realized it becomes, is a pretext for the staging of a shadow world of perversity that is hidden beneath the idealized surface or veneer of orthodox values.[10] Hitchcock's cinematic exhibitionism, his revelation/concealment of human perversity, is not something hidden in his work, something that requires, say a psychoanalytic theory to diagnose, for it is dramatized or staged in his art, made manifest through the aesthetic strategies that have become synonymous with Hitchcock's art: visual expressionism, self conscious "performativity," black humor, and suspense. *The Lodger*, Hitchcock's third film, is the first to fully articulate his aesthetic.

The Lodger: *Novel to Film*

Hitchcock's first re-working of the Jekyll/Ripper myth is profoundly indebted to the book from which the film was adapted, written in 1913 by Catholic writer Marie Belloc Lowndes (brother of Hillaire Belloc). Belloc Lowndes's *The Lodger* sold more than half a million copies and was turned into a successful London stage production—*Who is He?*—that Hitchcock attended.[11] The Jekyll/Ripper myth lies at the heart of the book. It is quoted directly by Daisy, the heroine of the novel, from a letter written to a newspaper editor: "It seems to me very probable that The Avenger—to give him the name by which he apparently wishes to be known—comprises in his own person the peculiarities of Jekyll and Hyde, Mr. Louis Stevenson's now famous hero."[12] Belloc Lowndes's novel is organized around the conceit that the Avenger is an aristocratic gentlemen who resides in a boarding house close to the crimes. The character of the Lodger in both Belloc Lowndes's book and Hitchcock's film conforms to John Ruskin's mid-nineteenth-century idea of a gentleman. "A gentleman's first characteristic," Ruskin writes "is that fineness of structure in the body, which renders it capable of the most delicate sensation; and of structure in the mind which renders it capable of the most delicate sympathies—one may say, simply, 'fineness of nature.' " He continues: "And, though rightness of moral conduct is ultimately the great purifier of race, the sign of nobleness is not in this rightness of moral conduct but in sensitiveness. When the make of the creature is fine, its temptations are strong as well as its perceptions; it is liable to all kinds of impressions in their most violent form; liable therefore to be abused and hurt by all kinds of rough things which would do a coarser creature little harm, and thus to fall into frightful wrong if its fate would have it so."[13] Jekyll/Ripper in Belloc Lowndes's novel is a man of acute and refined sensibility. The conceit that he resides as a lodger with ordinary people, allows Belloc Lowndes to explore the peculiar sympathy his difference solicits. Belloc Lowndes's singular contribution to the Jekyll/ Ripper myth—and to Hitchcock's career—is that she domesticates that myth; she brings the sensational into the domain of the familial and the ordinary in the manner that Hitchcock was later to claim for his television show.[14]

The psychological drama of Belloc Lowndes's book turns on the fact that while the proprietor of the lodgings, the kindly Mrs. Bunting, increasingly suspects that the Lodger is the Avenger, her instinct is to take the burden of this knowledge upon herself and to protect the Lodger from exposure to preserve his shameful secret. As she gathers all the circumstantial evidence necessary to implicate him in the crimes, she warns him not to go out because there are so many police about, and at the end of the novel, when she believes without doubt that he is the Avenger, she passively abets his escape. Mrs. Bunting's reticence, despite increasing evidence, to admit that the Lodger is the Avenger, stems from two sources. The Buntings are retired from service in an era when service is dying out. Mrs. Bunting's relationship to the upper-class lodger whom she harbors manifests the residue of class allegiance of servants to those they served, intensified, perhaps, by the fact that the Bunting's have rather lost their bearings trying to make their own way in the world. Mrs. Bunting becomes increasingly anxious about taking money from the Lodger, as if it were wrong to charge a young gentlemen to stay in one's house.

Mrs. Bunting's class allegiance is augmented by maternal/ feminine feelings, the desire to care for and protect this gentle, good-looking young man, to preserve him from a cruel and hostile world. These feelings exist in spite of her awareness of the Lodger's hatred toward women: "It hadn't taken the landlady very long to find out that her lodger had a queer kind of fear and dislike of woman. When she was doing the staircase and landings she would often hear Mr. Sleuth reading aloud to himself passages in the Bible that were very uncomplimentary to her sex. But Mrs. Bunting had no great opinion of her sister woman, so that it didn't put her out. Besides, where one's lodger is concerned, a dislike of women is better than—well, than the other thing."[15] It is not hard to conclude from this passage that the Lodger's indifference to women actually endears the Lodger to her and hence to think that their relationship resembles nothing so much as the relationship between an overprotective mother and her homosexual son. The word "queer" is used repeatedly in the novel to describe the Lodger. It ostensibly denotes "odd," "strange," or "eccentric," which are words also applied to him. Yet in the culture of post-Wildean England, the use of "queer" to describe a man of dandified appearance who is averse to women inevitably raises the specter of "abnormal" sexual proclivities, that is, homosexuality.[16]

The implications of Mrs. Bunting's allegiance to her lodger are dramatized through the presence in the story of a policeman, Joe Chandler, who comes to the house courting Mrs. Bunting's step-daughter, Daisy. On one occasion he arrives dressed in uniform and loudly jokes at the doorway that he is issuing a warrant for an arrest of the Lodger. Joe does not in fact suspect the Lodger, but his action serves to externalize and dramatize Mrs. Bunting's barely expressed or expressible anxieties. In the context of Mrs. Bunting's by now rather old-fashioned sense of class allegiance, the police represent an external, intrusive force. It should be remembered that the police were created in the mid-nineteenth century using recruits from the working classes by and for the new middle class who were prepared to trade some personal freedom for public safety, rather than by and for an aristocracy who were not traditionally beholden to such an institution. Working-class Joe represents this new social order that intrudes into Mrs. Bunting's complicit class relationship with the Lodger. But his intervention also carries the weight of a paternal law that acts as a counterweight to aristocratic effeminacy and sexual deviance supported and sustained by the servile Mrs. Bunting. Toward the end of the novel, Mrs. Bunting comes to identify with the Avenger's victims: "Up to now she had given very little thought—if indeed, any thought—to the drink sodden victims of The Avenger. It was he who had filled her thoughts,—he and those who were trying to track him down."[17] However, this belated discovery only intensifies her sympathy for the Avenger, for she experiences on his behalf a sense of guilt (transference of guilt): "The Avenger's acts came over Mrs. Bunting in a great seething flood of sick fear and—and, yes, remorse."[18]

Belloc Lowndes was a society lady as well as a popular novelist whose career was launched by none other than W.T. Stead, a lifelong friend. She was also an intimate of Constance Wilde, Oscar Wilde's wife, since her family had known Wilde's parents. Her comments on Constance and Oscar reveal a sense in which the circumstances surrounding the arrest, trial, and imprisonment of Wilde are germane to Belloc Lowndes's particular interpretation of the Jekyll/Ripper myth:

I was told by a friend, who did everything in her power to help them both, when it came to their day of shame and misery, that Constance was completely

ignorant of Oscar's other life. To her he had always
been the courteous, affectionate and indeed, devoted,
husband whom the more simple of her friends, myself
amongst them, envied her, and the more fearful must
have been her awakening when it be remembered
that, at the time Oscar Wilde was arrested, he had
become the most popular playwright of his day. I
have little doubt that he had her in mind when he
put into the mouth of one of his characters in *An Ideal
Husband* the words: "Women are not meant to judge,
but to forgive us when we need forgiveness. Pardon,
not punishment, is their mission."[19]

Belloc Lowndes's experience of the Wilde affair from the
perspective, as it were, of Constance surely informs her
portrayal of the Lodger, as someone who, from the class and
maternal-feminine standpoint of Mrs. Bunting, requires
nurturing and protection.

Hitchcock and his collaborators Eliot Stannard
(screenplay) and Alma Hitchcock (assistant director) follow
Mrs. Bunting's arc of growing suspicion in the novel about
her "queer" lodger. He makes a suspicious request to have
pictures of young women removed from his bedroom walls,
as if they stare at him with recriminating glances; he
mysteriously paces the room; Mrs. Bunting discovers a
locked cabinet which we know to contain a bag suspiciously
like the one that is said to be carried by the Avenger; and we
experience the Lodger's nocturnal departure into the London
fog through the point of view of Mrs. Bunting, alone and
wide awake, pensively listening at her bedroom door.[20]
However, Hitchcock's film falls short of making Mrs. Bunting
complicit in the Lodger's actions in the manner of the novel.
In the novel, unlike the film, Mrs. Bunting discovers the
Lodger's map but conceals her discovery.

Furthermore, the film transforms Belloc Lowndes's story
by introducing Daisy as the daughter of the Buntings, who
falls in love with the Lodger, now set up as a rival to Joe,
and steadfastly believes in his innocence. In the novel the

romance between Joe and Daisy takes back seat to the
murder-mystery plot that focuses on the mother's suspicions
of the Lodger, as befits the class and matriarchal focus of the
novel. In the light of Hitchcock's subsequent career in
America, one can imagine the appeal to Hitchcock of
retaining the focus on the mother figure harboring a
psychotic son-figure with the heroine either being killed (as
in *Psycho*, 1960) or marrying the cop (as in *Shadow of a Doubt*,
1943). However, faced with a studio reluctant to cast Novello
as Jack the Ripper, Hitchcock and his collaborators created a
love story between Daisy and the Lodger that displaced the
class-matriarchal focus as a source of rival authority to the
law in favor of a romance narrative, which, with or without
the theme of class mobility, became so central to his *oeuvre*.
In this way (perhaps as much by circumstance as by design)
Hitchcock created a "wrong-man" narrative in which the
criminal of the murder-mystery doubles as the hero of the
romance plot, thereby consolidating the formula that he was
to use throughout his career.[21] The heroine's desire for the
hero who is a criminal suspect dramatizes romance in
oedipal, Freudian terms, as something that challenges the
authority of the law linked to paternal authority.

The love story in the film is completely at odds with the
hermeneutics of suspicion that characterizes Mrs. Bunting's
attitude toward the Lodger. For if Daisy is right in falling in
love with the Lodger—and how could she be so radically
misguided?—then the Lodger is in fact a romantic hero and
not the menacing figure he appears to be. The opening of the
narrative frames our expectations, but it frames those
expectations falsely. Shots of a model and a member of the
public masquerading as the Avenger with dark muffler and
hat prime the audience to recognize the Lodger as the
Avenger when he arrives at the Buntings' household. But the
opening sequence also demonstrates the power of the mass
media in whipping up public hysteria about the Lodger and
engendering false accusations: anyone could be the Avenger.
Just as Mrs. Bunting does in part succumb to a mass media
scare, we the audience are duped in a similar way by

Hitchcock's film. Narrative events that appear to signal the presence of consummate evil turn out to be benign. His aversion to the pictures of young women, the map he possesses of the killings, his nocturnal activities: all these, it turns out, can be explained by the fact that the Avenger killed his sister and, keeping his word to his mother, the Lodger is avenging her death by tracking down the killer. At the end of the film the Lodger becomes the archetypal "wrong man" pursued through the streets by the raging mob in a scene that echoes the actual pursuit of the wrong man, Leather Apron, in the wake of the Ripper murders, and almost lynched by the mob in a scene that evokes the crucifixion.

But the nature of the changes that Hitchcock and his collaborators made to the novel is not simply to dramatize competing and incompatible points of view of the Lodger's actions within the narrative, but also to alter the relationship between reader/spectator and the characters and events in the text. For the question at stake in Belloc Lowndes's novel is not whether the Lodger is really the Avenger nor whether the Lodger is a sympathetic character. Rather, the focus of the novel is how Mrs. Bunting responds to her growing knowledge that the Lodger is the Avenger, and her complicity in maintaining the gentleman's secret, her reasons for harboring the Lodger in spite of his guilt. Narrative suspense is subservient to the development of character psychology, that is, to bestowing a level of depth and complexity to character. However, in Hitchcock's film, the dimension of sympathy for the Lodger no longer derives from complicity with a criminal but from Daisy's belief that the Lodger is innocent. Rather than exploring the complex and ambiguous motivation of one (or more) characters, Hitchcock creates competing unambiguous points of view, both contradictory and undecidable, that focus on the identity of the Lodger. Is the Lodger an innocent victim or is he the Avenger? Is he a figure of threat or sympathy? Is he is a gentleman or he is a sexual predator? Either Mrs. Bunting or Daisy may be deceiving themselves about the Lodger, but Hitchcock is not interested in exploring motivation. Depth in Hitchcock's film is a matter of surface, as it were. Ambiguity resides not in the motivations of character but in visual narration, in the legibility of appearances. The pleasures of narrative suspense are not subservient to moral insight, as in Belloc Lowndes's novel, but become an end in themselves. A deadly serious question—"Is the Lodger a psychotic killer?"—becomes for Hitchcock a source of entertainment, a macabre joke. It's not that these moments of doubt about the Lodger aren't scary, but Hitchcock recognizes that we enjoy being entertained by their scariness. It is fun to think that the Lodger might be a psychotic killer.

Visual Narration in The Lodger

The primacy of Hitchcock's ludic visual narration over his solicitation of audience identification with character is secured by Hitchcock's use of visual expressionism and the Kuleshov effect. Both visual expressionism and Soviet montage emphasized the idea that the film image was an artificial creation whose content and design could be thoroughly and completely controlled by the artist. This idea was congenial to Hitchcock both on account of his facility as a graphic artist and because of his growing identification with the director as the supreme authority in the film-making process. By the time he made The Lodger in 1925 Hitchcock was familiar with German expressionism not only from screenings of German films at the London Film Society but also through his practical exposure to Weimar film-making during his residence in Berlin, where in 1924 he worked as a set designer for film director Graham Cutts on his film The Blackguard (1925), closely observed German film director F.W. Murnau at work on The Last Laugh (1924), and had the opportunity to absorb himself in German film culture.

Hitchcock's re-telling of the Ripper myth in The Lodger is closely informed by the rhetoric of visual expressionism, particularly in Wiene's The Cabinet of Dr. Caligari (1919), Murnau's Nosferatu (1922), and Leni's Waxworks (1924), one of whose three sections is a narrative of Jack the Ripper.[22] These films draw upon the German romantic tradition of Heinrich von Kleist and E.T.A. Hoffmann in which an ordinary middle-class milieu is doubled by another world peopled with nightmare figures possessed with power over life and death that is both demonic and seductive.

In Murnau's adaptation of the story of Dracula, the vampire infiltrates Bremen of the Biedermeier era and the relationship between the hero and heroine of the film, as a figure of death. In Wiene's *Cabinet of Dr. Caligari*, Caligari doubles as a respectable Doctor in command of a lunatic asylum and an itinerant circus entertainer who harbors and controls a murderous somnambulist, Cesare, who stalks the local town and commits a series of brutal murders. In the Ripper episode of Leni's *Waxworks*, the narrator dreams that, as he makes love to his girlfriend, Jack the Ripper, or "Spring Heeled Jack," intervenes and takes her from him. By making Jack a figment of the narrator's imagination and a spectral presence in the *mise-en-scène*, Leni suggests that Jack serves to represent or double the narrator's own unacknowledged desires. The narrative style of expressionism, especially the use of starkly contrasting light and shadow, stylized *mise-en-scène*, non-naturalistic acting, elliptical narration, and, in the case of Murnau and Leni, trick photography served to dramatize the sense of a world of otherness that lies within or alongside the ordinary world of appearances.[23]

However it should also be noted that Hitchcock's association of Jekyll-Ripper with the figure of a vampire, while influenced by the rhetoric of German expressionist cinema, is part of a much broader literary tradition in which the aristocrat is linked to the predatory vampire. From its inception as a literary phenomenon in Polidori's *Vampire* (1819), and popularized in the anonymously published, *Varney the Vampire* (1847), the figure of the vampire was portrayed as an aristocratic libertine or rake, typically of foreign ancestry, who became a phantom ruler of the night preying upon defenseless, virginal women.

The literary tradition of vampirism, of course, culminated in the nineteenth century with the publication of Bram Stoker's *Dracula* in 1897, but even before the publication of *Dracula*, Jack the Ripper, conceived as an aristocrat, was already being cast in the role of the vampire. A striking cartoon in *Punch* portrayed Jack the Ripper as a ghoulish knife-wielding phantom of death, with preternatural gifts of perception. This popular conception of the Ripper as a phantom is given a literary inflection in a police report by one Detective White, documented by Donald Rumbelow:

> His face was long and thin, nostrils rather delicate, and his hair was jet black. His complexion was inclined to be sallow, and altogether the man was foreign in appearance. The most striking thing about him, however, was the extraordinary brilliance of his eyes. They looked like two very luminous glow worms coming through the darkness. . . . His hands were snow white, and the fingers long and tapering. As the man passed me at the lamp I had an uneasy feeling there was something more than unusually sinister about him.[24]

This report is remarkable not only in the way it is so deeply informed by a literary culture, but also in the manner it prefigures Hitchcock's own portrayal of Jack the Ripper in *The Lodger*.[25]

The influence of Soviet montage and in particular, Eisenstein, upon Hitchcock is less direct than German expressionism, but equally significant. Hitchcock probably read about the Kuleshov effect in the writings of Pudovkin on film that were translated into English in 1928 by Ivor Montagu, the young cineaste and founding member of the London Film Society, and Hitchcock's thoughts upon the idea of "pure cinema," first articulated in the early 1930s, clearly demonstrate his indebtedness to Eisenstein's early essays on film. However, Hitchcock could not have had access to these texts before he made *The Lodger* in 1926. Hitchcock reports in an

interview for *Close Up* magazine in 1930 that he had seen
Battleship Potemkin (1925), but that it was the only Russian
film he had seen.[26] Furthermore, since the film had been
banned by the censors, its British premiere, which took place
at the London Film Society, did not occur until November 10,
1929. This was probably the occasion on which Hitchcock
saw it, long after the completion of *The Lodger*.[27]

Potemkin premiered in Berlin on April 29, 1926, and began
a successful run in the German capital, but it is highly
unlikely that Hitchcock saw the film there because he began
shooting *The Lodger* at the beginning of May and production
lasted into July.[28] However, Montagu, who was working for
the *Times* of London, met up with Eisenstein, Alexandrov,
and Tisse during their European tour after the completion of
Potemkin. Montagu was with them first in Paris and then in
Berlin where they arrived in March.[29] The Russian travelers
left Berlin three days before the premiere of the film, but it
is quite likely that Montagu would have stayed on to see it.
Once he had arrived back in England, he was invited by
Michael Balcon, Hitchcock's producer, to re-edit *The Lodger*,
which meanwhile had received a disastrous studio screening.
Montagu re-edited the film in early September. It is
reasonable to conclude that the Eisensteinian influence
that seems so evident in the film derives in part from
Montagu, fresh from his firsthand experiences with
Eisenstein and a viewing of *Potemkin*. Yet, even without this
direct connection, Hitchcock was indirectly exposed to the
influence of the Russian filmmakers through the movies of
the French avant-garde that were regularly screened at the
film society.

Hitchcock learned a number of lessons from the Soviet
filmmakers. First, Hitchcock learned from the Soviets, as he
learned from Murnau, to treat the organization of the image
as a form of graphic design in which the meaning of every
element could be controlled, even as an event was being
acted and staged within it. The visual design of the film
image allowed Hitchcock to create meanings that expanded
upon or even conflicted with the meanings denoted by

dramatic action, intertitles, or dialogue. Second, the Kuleshov effect, an approach to editing that emphasized the creation of meanings through the juxtaposition of images in a manner that exceeded the meanings conveyed by any given shot in isolation, allowed Hitchcock to augment the level of connoted meaning contained within an image across a series of images. Third, the Soviet filmmaker's attention to the juxtaposition of images for their own sake rather than for the sake of narrative progression allowed Hitchcock to deploy the montage techniques in the creation of narrative suspense, considered not simply as the postulation of an alternative narrative outcome but as a retardation or delay in narrative development, specifically a delay in establishing or resolving the romance. Finally, Hitchcock's interest in these techniques, like his interest in German expressionism, was not simply formal or stylistic but thematic. That is, the creation of connotation and metaphor through the design and juxtaposition of images, together with the use of montage to delay narrative outcome, is frequently in Hitchcock related in a very Freudian way to the presence of hidden, obscene, or perverse meaning. And this connection, if it was not learned from Eisenstein's films, nonetheless demonstrates a close affinity with Eisenstein's own predilection for hidden, perverse meanings.

Visual expressionism and Hitchcock's distinctive use of the Kuleshov effect come together in the sequence that introduces the Lodger (Ivor Novello) to the Buntings and to the viewer. The Lodger arrives at the door of the Bunting house (number 13) just after the announcement of another Avenger murder in the vicinity. The camera assumes the perceptual point of view of the Lodger as he approaches the front door whose frame bears the shape of a cross that is obscured by his advancing shadow, in a manner that at once registers the threatening presence of the Lodger and renders secret his identity. At the moment Mrs. Bunting opens the door to the Lodger, Joe is stealing a kiss from Daisy in the kitchen and Mr. Bunting is trying to repair the cuckoo clock in the hall, precariously balanced on a chair. Hitchcock cuts

from a full shot behind Mrs. Bunting as she begins to open
the door to a medium shot of the same action and back to a
full shot again as she completes and continues the movement, prolonging the moment of suspense, of revelation, for
the viewer and leaving the appearance of the Lodger suggested
but not yet disclosed. Hitchcock then cuts to a close-up of
Mrs. Bunting's bewildered, if not horrified, reaction before
finally revealing to us in close-up the piercing eyes of the
Lodger, his face half concealed by a dark scarf. After a second
reaction shot of Mrs. Bunting, Hitchcock cuts to a point-of-view
medium shot of the Lodger revealing his snow-white hand
and long, tapering fingers resting languidly on his breast.

Given the way that the audience has been primed to
expect the appearance of the Lodger, we are dying to see
what the figure who arrives at Mrs. Bunting's door looks
like. Hitchcock deploys an Eisensteinian extension of screen
time over story time through montage editing in order to
tease the audience and inflame our desire to see.[30] By
delaying our gratification in this way, Hitchcock is playing a
mildly sadistic joke with the audience, a sadism muted by
the fact that twice before we have watched individuals act as
the Lodger while others are duped momentarily by the
masquerade. Hitchcock has thus made the audience complicit
in the game of black humor he is playing. This complicity
places us in a position that is strikingly at odds with the
viewpoint of the nervous Mrs. Bunting. Mrs. Bunting is fascinated by the figure in the doorway, and the audience is
fascinated by the figure, too. However, because our desire to
see what the Avenger looks like has been primed by
Hitchcock and we are conscious of being thus primed, the
presence in the frame of Mrs. Bunting, who does not have
the distance we have from what she sees, allows us to see in
her our own naive selves and to take pleasure in the scene at
a safe distance. By staging in this way Mrs. Bunting's
response to the apparition of the Lodger, Hitchcock invites
us to savor a confrontation that is a source of alarm for the
character, and to be delighted by the thought that Novello is
a murderous sexual predator.

The presence of Novello in the scene further contributes to its staging for the spectator (in contrast to Mrs. Bunting). By the time he made *The Lodger*, Novello was well established as a matinee idol. In Griffith's *The White Rose* (1923) he plays a passionate aristocratic southerner whose brief affair with a working class girl leaves her pregnant, yet when he discovers her plight he proves honorable in the end and marries her. In Cutts's *The Rat* (1925) he plays a denizen of Berlin's criminal underworld, a rogue and a charmer, who nonetheless retains his sense of honor. Novello's star persona in Cutts's film (obviously trading off the popularity of Valentino) is a highly self-conscious performance of roguishness that emphasizes the underlying lovability of his character. When the Lodger first appears in Hitchcock's film, the audience is primed less to recognize Jack the Ripper than to recognize and appreciate Novello's "stage entrance."

Audience familiarity with Novello as the lovable rogue provides immunization against the thought that he really is "Jack the Ripper," yet at the same time, it also provides grounds for the audience to entertain the thought that Novello plays a character of unspeakable perversity. And it is surely no accident that Hitchcock chose an actor rumored or known to be homosexual to enact this role, even if the fact was not widely known. Furthermore, the knowledgeable audience will recognize that the Lodger's phantom-like presence emerging out of the London fog resembles *Nosferatu* and that Mrs. Bunting's reaction recalls the astonishment of the heroine of *The Cabinet of Dr. Caligari* when Caligari as showman reveals to her the rigid body of the phallic somnambulist lying down in the coffin-like "cabinet." In other words, Novello's performance also involves a self-conscious allusion to expectations set up outside the film about the nature of the monstrous, with the connotations of perversity these allusions carry with them. In this way the idea of the monstrous in the Lodger becomes a self-conscious effect of its overall staging that includes the performance of Novello. As a result, the moment of monstrous revelation is safe to enjoy because monstrous perversion remains entirely concealed behind the "aestheticized" surface of staging and performance.

The appearance of the Lodger at the door of the Buntings' is also framed by the action of Daisy's aging father who goes to the hallway to climb up on a chair to repair the cuckoo clock just before the doorbell rings. The idea suggested by Hitchcock here that the clock has stopped, that time is in some way out of joint, is one that recurs in his work, and in *Rear Window* (1954) it is, of course, Hitchcock himself who winds the clock in his cameo appearance. The idea that time, symbolically, stands still at the moment of the Lodger's entrance underscores the way in which his entrance is an interruption of the normal order of things, of the temporal routine of the ordinary life. Furthermore, after the Lodger arrives Mr. Bunting precipitously falls off his chair as if consecution entailed consequence, as if the fact that the fall occurs after the Lodger's arrival entails that the fall occurred *because* of the Lodger's arrival. The noise of his precipitous fall causes Daisy to end her surreptitious love-making with Joe in the kitchen and rush out to help him. In this way, the interruption of time is linked by Hitchcock to a literal staging of the displacement of the father and the suspension of romance. The Lodger reacts in a pensive almost paranoid way to the sound of the cuckoo (conventionally both a disruptive, mocking noise and an allusion to transgressive sexual behavior) that is released as if in response to the father's fall, and his wide-eyed, pensive response continues, as Daisy, bent over her father, giggles at his predicament in a manner that connects her to the bird and to the Lodger's response to it.

The scene that is perhaps the most emblematic of Hitchcock's staging of perversion in *The Lodger* and is certainly the most complex occurs when Hitchcock teases the audience with the idea that Joe, too, has qualities of character like Jekyll/Ripper. Earlier when making love to Daisy, Joe asserts, "I'm keen on golden hair myself, same as the Avenger is." Now Joe declares that when he has put a noose around the Lodger's neck, he will put a ring around Daisy's finger. And he proceeds to chase her playfully with a ring that takes the form of a pair of handcuffs. The chase proceeds into the hallway where, at the foot of the stairs, Joe places the handcuffs on Daisy. Suddenly Daisy panics hysterically as if the game were real, as if Joe's darker intentions toward her have been unmasked in his actions. Meanwhile, the Lodger, alerted by the noise, appears at the top of the stairs and rushes out of his room, his shadow cast on the wall of the landing against the ominous expressionistic shadows of the banister. Perched at the top of the stairs he peers down from on high upon the struggling couple, his chest heaving, but he does nothing to intervene; rather he contemplates the scene. Mrs. Bunting rushes down the stairs past him to comfort Daisy, and the Lodger looks on in apparent disdain at the bemused Joe, who is left alone at the foot of the stairs holding the handcuffs, and, one is inclined to interpret, rendered impotent by events.

The actions in this scene contain such a wealth of details that they are almost illegible, and the meaning of the scene is opaque. This opacity serves to underscore the sense of perversion that, as Hitchcock pointed out to Truffaut, prompted the use of the handcuffs.[31] Joe is likened to the Avenger, and his approach is at once courted and rebuffed by Daisy. Yet her reaction to the game is an over-reaction that suggests both her fear and desire with respect to sexuality. But how are we to understand the response of the Lodger? Ostensibly he rushes out because he hears Daisy's screams, but why is his action shrouded in expressionism? Is he rushing to help or drawn to witness? His chest heaves. Why? In anger or because he is aroused? He is contemptuous of the lugubrious Joe. Why? Because what Joe is doing is simply ungentlemanly, or that it is not gentlemanly enough, that is it is not, as it were fully realized or aestheticized? By placing the Lodger in the scene, Hitchcock allows us to see the struggle with the handcuffs through the eyes of a third party whose response to the struggle is as ambiguous as the struggle itself. Like the "third party" staging of Mrs. Bunting's encounter with the Lodger in the doorway of the house, we are invited to take perverse pleasure in contemplating the scene between Joe and Daisy. However here our pleasure is licensed by a third party within the scene, rather than by Hitchcock himself: the Lodger acts as Hitchcock's delegate within the fiction. Here the Lodger's gaze seems to stand in for Hitchcock's gaze. The Lodger's ambiguous response cues and authorizes us to take perverse pleasure in a scene that on its own we could not ''afford'' to enjoy on our own.

The ways in which Hitchcock's visual narration dramatically exceeds character point of view and inscribes perversity into the portrayal of romance is further illustrated in his portrayal of the relationship between Daisy and the Lodger, which evolves as a romance to the point of a kiss, and ultimately, the film suggests, a marriage, and yet at the same time remains stuck in the repetitious staging of incipient perversion.

When Daisy brings the Lodger his breakfast they are in close proximity for the first time. In close-up we see the Lodger pick up a knife from the breakfast table, followed by a close-up profile of the Lodger that, as Rothman notes, precludes access to the character's interiority.[32] But we also see a gleam of light on the Lodger's teeth, as his mouth is frozen slightly open. Beneath the controlled, opaque, mask-like veneer, the shot suggests, may lie a chaotic murderous desire. It turns out that the Lodger uses the knife, innocently, to flick an unsightly speck (of food?) from Daisy's clothing. But even this gesture is ambiguous in the manner that it reinforces Daisy's status as a fetish object, an idealized image of perfection, from which all stains or blemishes must be removed.

In a subsequent scene Daisy and the Lodger play chess in front of a fireplace whose rainbow arch, as Lesley Brill argues, links them in romance.[33] But as Daisy reaches to pick up a chess piece we see that the Lodger, unknown to her, has picked up a poker that is poised in the frame close to her head, and we imagine a frightful continuation of the gesture.[34] At this moment, Hitchcock cuts to Joe's arrival at

the house. He has just been put on the Avenger case. When
we return to the couple, the Lodger is stoking a raging fire
with his poker. He puts the poker down and impulsively
reaches to caress Daisy's hair. "Beautiful Golden Hair" he
says, and they look into each other's eyes before they
nervously pull back and the camera withdraws to a less
intimate distance.

Later on, after Mrs. Bunting's suspicions have been
aroused by his nocturnal wanderings, the Lodger arises from
perusing a map of the murders and looks out of the window
on the rain. Pensively he turns toward the camera as if he
has resolved upon course of action. Hitchcock cuts to a
medium side view of Daisy in the bath with steam arising
from it that begins a series of cross cuts between Daisy and
the Lodger: close-up of the Lodger clasping the doorknob of
the bathroom—it is locked; cut to Daisy's feet splashing in
the water, seen from above, and back to the side view of
Daisy in the bath; cut to medium shot of the Lodger in
thought with a wry smile creeping upon his face; cut to
close-up glamour profile of Daisy; cut back to reaction shot
of the Lodger; cut to profile shot of Daisy, and then a shot of
her feet in the bath water from above; cut back to the Lodger
who, it seems, reluctantly and ruefully withdraws from the
door. The Lodger then turns as if on an entirely different
pretext and motivation, knocks, and inquires of Daisy
whether he has offended her with the present he brought in
a previous scene. In tone and content the sequence is an
uncanny anticipation of *Psycho* . . . *Psycho interruptus*.

Toward the end of the film, believing that Daisy is in
grave danger, Joe has followed the Lodger and Daisy during
their nocturnal assignation. Rebuffed, he comes to the
conclusion that the Lodger is the Avenger. Meanwhile the
Lodger takes Daisy to his room. As they move to embrace he
seems distracted by her golden curls and Hitchcock cuts
downstairs to the worried mother comforted by the father.
Back upstairs in full shot the couple are laughing; then
Hitchcock cuts abruptly to a close up of Daisy looking
longingly at the Lodger followed by a close-up of the Lodger

as his face approaches the screen very slowly into extreme close-up, his rouged lips looming into the camera like the lips of a vampire. Again his embrace is deflected and deferred by the sight of her hair, as if his impulse to action is frozen in the presence of this fetish, as if to consummate his desire would be to debase it. When they finally kiss, the kiss is ethereal and idealized. Meanwhile, downstairs the father anxiously looks at his watch (again connecting paternal impotence with a failure to control time). Hitchcock cuts back to the couple as the Lodger rebuffs her in front of two oval portraits on the wall that seem to stare at him accusingly.

In the final scene of the film, after the Lodger has been exonerated and the real murderer has reportedly been caught, the couple embrace on the staircase of the Lodger's mansion, but outside the window a neon sign flashes "TO-NIGHT GOLDEN CURLS," a sign whose earlier display in the film signaled the promise of the dance revue, the promise of romance, and the promise of incipient murder. As the parents relish their daughter's new-found status, trying out the Lodger's plush furniture for size, the camera closes in on the kiss. At the conclusion of the shot Daisy nestles in the Lodger's shoulder, and he gazes at her blonde hair as his rouged lips part in a smile that reveals his gleaming white teeth. Some have read the scene as establishing conclusively the innocence of the Lodger. For example, Charles Barr writes:

> As the parents withdraw and the couple embrace, we can see behind them, deep in the shot beyond the window, the same sign, "TO-NIGHT GOLDEN CURLS," now located for the first time within the film's own space and diminished in size. The camera moves in on them and excludes the sign from the frame. The film has gone from a woman's scream to a woman's happy smile; from a sign with menacing and provocative overtones, to a sign that seems, at least for the moment, made safe, and given a new meaning; from a night of murder to the promise of a night of love.[35]

However, it seems to me that the meaning of the sign cannot be neutralized so easily. While the containment of the sign in the image and its displacement by the embracing couple anchors its reference to the love making of the Lodger and Daisy, it is not thereby divested of all the connotations that it has accrued during the course of the film. These connotations are merely transferred, irrevocably, to their final embrace.

The status of Hitchcock's visual narration in these scenes has been a source of controversy in critical responses to *The Lodger* ever since Lindsay Anderson dismissed the aspersions cast on the motivation of the Lodger as an "illegitimate" distraction from the main plot.[36] Brill warns against exaggerating the "mildly ironic suggestions of tarnish" on the character of the Lodger, or it will render the central themes of the film incoherent. To equate the Avenger with the hero, he writes, asks us to forget that the former is a madman who has killed innocent young women and that the latter is the grieving brother of one of its victims.[37] But in contesting a reductively ironic interpretation of the film—the Lodger is really no different from the Avenger—Brill minimizes the force of the irony whose presence he elsewhere wishes to acknowledge and he misunderstands the constitutive ambiguity that characterizes the portrayal of romance in Hitchcock's work. *The Lodger* is a film that is structurally ambiguous or undecidable in a manner that is a defining characteristic of many of Hitchcock's films rather than a supplementary feature to be dismissed or avoided on account of the fact that it produces apparent inconsistency.[38]

Throughout *The Lodger*, as I have shown, Hitchcock uses a silent film aesthetic of visual expressionism and montage—either within the shot, in Eisenstein's sense of creating semantic conflict or ambiguity within the image, or between shots—to create a visual pun that allows us to entertain perverse thoughts about what the Lodger would like to do to Daisy. Silent visual representation, without the clarification and explanation of what it is that we see provided by sound and dialogue, lends itself to ambiguity, although of course ambiguity can be sustained in dialogue through *double entendre*. Since in silent film the burden of sustaining character and character motivation rests heavily upon easily understood conventions of gesture and behavior, of type, it can thus be readily used to expose the conventions of gesture and behavior as something that are merely a surface phenomenon. The thought we are consistently invited to entertain about the Lodger is that beneath his gentlemanly surface he is a murderous sexual predator. Like a sophisticated schoolboy, Hitchcock titillates the audience with the thought of perversion, the force of the joke at once expressed and contained, like the Freudian joke, by being displaced into visual style and contained within a moment of narrative suspense. This lies at the basis of what I would term Hitchcock's queer aesthetic, in which the conventional romance that is the ostensible subject matter or script of his films is sabotaged by narrative doubling, supported and sustained through a ludic, commentative, and self-conscious visual narration, that retards, delays, renders self-consciously fictive, and sometimes undermines completely the promise of heterosexual union. In the case of *The Lodger*, as with many of Hitchcock's works, it is as if the romance plot exists in order to stage aestheticized expressions of perverse desire that are ostensibly antithetical to it.

The Epistemology of the Closet

Hitchcock offers, retrospectively, to explain the ambiguity away by proposing an account of the Lodger's secret that is not one of a repressed and murderous sexuality. Yet, as William Rothman and Ken Mogg have argued, the Lodger's confession to Daisy of his painful secret is staged in such a way as to only compound the ambiguity that is attached to it.[39] The secret the gentleman purportedly reveals to Daisy in the flashback is that he is a man haunted by the death a woman—his sister—and after her, the deaths of all the women who have been murdered by the Avenger. It is this proximity of the Lodger to the death of young women that causes him to turn the pictures of the women in his room to face the wall, and it is also what makes him so intensely responsive to Daisy and her beauty. Daisy is something to be cherished, preserved, and adored. In this story, the heterosexual romance is idealized and etherialized. It issues, we surmise, from the special bond that exists between a brother and sister broken asunder by a cruel and gratuitous murder, and is renewed in the Lodger's idealization of Daisy. It seems to explain the Lodger's—and Hitchcock's—idealization of the romance in the Lodger as one untainted by perverse desire. Or does it? The very desexualization of the motive of the Lodger's attachment to women, the sense in which it is driven rather by a higher moral purpose, by altruism, only serves to cast the very suspicion upon the nature of his attachment to Daisy that this explanation of his motive is supposed to resolve. The Lodger's sensibility appears too refined to be real.

The flashback of his sister's death is staged in such a way that it only inflames our suspicion. First, his confession is made to Daisy on the site of the cobbled square where the Avenger has killed the women of "golden curls" as if, his confession is, as it were, a substitution for the murder that would otherwise be taking place there. Second, his sister's murder, narrated in the flashback, takes place at the moment of her coming out ball, suggesting the moment of female sexual efflorescence. Why would the Avenger begin his murderous campaign here at this upper-class coming out ball that one cannot imagine has any personal significance if the Avenger were not the Lodger? Third, Hitchcock films the murder sequence in a manner that distances the audience; indeed, he films it in a manner that self-consciously suggests that what is depicted is something that is not simply narrated but "framed." In particular, the audience is precluded from seeing the murder, opening up the possibility that the Lodger did the deed himself.

After a Rossetti-like image of a girl with "golden curls" appears superimposed on the face of the Lodger as he begins his confession, Hitchcock cuts to a medium shot of the

Lodger dancing with his sister at the ball. The camera then withdraws behind but continues to peer through an elaborate art deco doorway. Hitchcock cuts again to the Lodger and his sister dancing, and then cuts to a long shot of the dancers, who are seen framed within the frame of the film at the top of a staircase as two dancers leave. An unknown hand (the hand of the director?) emerges in an insert shot to kill the lights. We see them dim in long shot, and Hitchcock cuts to the sister's face in close-up, screaming (an image that has recurred through the film). Hands grapple to switch on the light and the camera "returns" through the art deco doorway to the scene of the crime and the body of the murdered woman. After his sister's death, the Lodger visits his mother's deathbed: "Swear to me, my son," she pleas, "you will not rest until The Avenger has been brought to justice." "Since then," the Lodger tells Daisy, now back in the present, "I have been tracking him down. Every week he moved nearer your street."

This sequence of events is entirely consistent with the idea that the Lodger is Jack the Ripper who murders his sister to take revenge upon her for her expression of a sexuality that he finds obscene and intolerable. The murderous act perhaps expresses the Lodger's refusal to allow her to become an object of heterosexual desire at the moment she is made into such an object, the refusal to allow the "virgin" to become, in the eyes of the Lodger *qua* Avenger, "a whore." And in this sense the murder of the sister is portrayed by Hitchcock's camera as a moment of ecstasy for the heroine, not simply sexual but spiritual, a moment of sanctification. This is a mirror image of those idealized moments of heterosexual embrace in the film that are stalked by connotations of death. Furthermore, the scene between the Lodger and his mother perhaps intimates, as Mogg suggests, a role for the mother in exacerbating the Lodger's "madness," in compelling and compounding a spiral of pursuit and being pursued, where the roles of pursuer and pursued are not simply roles allotted to characters in a wrong man narrative but suggest an internal pathology of self-division and self-hatred that receives its frankest, most undisguised expression in *Psycho*.

Hitchcock's narration in *The Lodger*, as we have seen, does not dwell on motive. The question of motive is occluded throughout the film in favor of the game Hitchcock has played as to whether or not the Lodger is the Avenger. Hitchcock's narration invites interpretation, it teases us to divine the nature of the secret he poses about the Lodger, but it entertains us with the question rather than exploring the answer. When in the flashback he finally proposes a solution to the puzzle of motive—that the Lodger witnessed a dreadful murder of the sister he loved—the solution only serves to suggest that which it denies. Indeed, it suggests that which it denies through denying or disguising it. Thus we are invited in the flashback to think that the Lodger has a different motive. In taking us back to origins, to a moment before the first murder and to the Lodger's family relationships, in particular his relationship with his mother, Hitchcock suggests to us, allusively, almost incoherently, not simply the fact that the Lodger is the Avenger, but what it is that motivates the Lodger, if he is indeed the Avenger. However, Hitchcock does not provide anything like an answer to this question: instead he uses the occasion to display the logic by which the secret about the Lodger has been maintained throughout the film.

Hitchcock's visual narration of the flashback shows or suggests more than the Lodger *qua* Avenger could possibly tell. "Truth" lies not in what can be rationally narrated about the Lodger's past, a narration which serves to assert the innocence of the wrong man and cement the romantic union, rather it lies in the contrived surface of Hitchcock's images, in what those images reveal through their concealment. While for the characters within his text, in particular Daisy, dissemblance is unmasked once and for all and the truth about the Lodger is revealed as something beneath the mysterious facade, for Hitchcock the narrator, the truth about the Lodger lies in the idealized, contrived surface of the film. It is, if you like, an effect of this surface.

In the course of her discussions of nineteenth- and early twentieth-century fiction, Eve Kosofsky Sedgwick identifies two contrasting types of literature that act as figurations what she terms the "epistemology of the closet" in which homosexual desire is denied existence in world of compulsory heterosexuality, other than as an unknown and unknowable secret. The first form of literature, the "paranoid gothic," exemplified by James Hogg's novel *Confessions of a Justified Sinner* (1824), and later, by Stevenson's *Dr. Jekyll and Mr. Hyde*, consists of narratives in which the fears and desires of the protagonist find their expression in the figure of a double, a source at once of persecution and fascination.[40]

The second form of literature is the bachelor literature of the late nineteenth and early twentieth century which features a sexually anesthetized hero exemplified in James's short story "The Beast in the Jungle" (1903). The hero of James's story, John Marcher, who is courted unrequitedly by Mary Bartram, harbors a secret "sense of being kept for something rare and strange, possibly prodigious and terrible, that was sooner or later to happen," the existence of which is itself denied or hidden. This "secret of having a secret," Sedgwick writes, "functions, in Marcher's life, precisely as the closet. It is not a closet in which there is a homosexual man, for Marcher is not a homosexual man. Instead, it is the closet of, simply, the homosexual secret—the closet of imagining a homosexual secret."[41] Marcher lives the life of a closeted person: "all that could in the least be called behavior," James writes, was "a long act of dissimulation," and this dissimulation includes, for Sedgwick, his ostensible heterosexuality.[42] Stevenson's *Dr. Jekyll and Mr. Hyde*, with its sexually anesthetized bachelor hero by day who also doubles as the bestial murderer by night, borrows from the second, as well as the first tradition.

James's sexually disinterested bachelor hero with a secret is not unlike the hero of Belloc Lowndes's novel. The Lodger lives like a closeted person, yet he embodies the qualities of Jekyll and Hyde, and the nature of his deeds are specifically motivated by an animus toward woman and their sexuality.

However, whereas Belloc Lowndes focuses on Mrs. Bunting's response to the truth of the Lodger's behavior, Hitchcock's narration, as we have seen, purposively and playfully preserves the structure of the secret, even at its moment of apparent resolution in the manner of James's evasive narration. Rather than deny the existence of the secret, like James, Hitchcock denies its resolution. And while conventional interpreters of Hitchcock, like conventional interpreters of James, see the truth of the story to reside in the hero's love for the heroine, Hitchcock's evasive narration, like the narration of James, suggests something else. The Lodger is in the closet; his life is an act of dissemblance. His sexual relationship to women, compelled by culture, is one in which women, in order to be loved, must be aestheticized, idealized, or etherialized, but their bodies or their sexuality are a source of disgust.

The scene of the "coming out" ball is a scene where heterosexual female sexuality is put on display for the male gaze (and for the spectator), but what actually "comes out" is masculine rage at female sexuality. This rage, of course, may have nothing to do with the Lodger, other than the fact that he happens to be the brother of the victim. Deniability about the Lodger's motivation is built into Hitchcock's narration, thereby preserving the structure of the secret. Yet the scene is contrived to invite us to think that the Lodger's involvement is much more intimate. After all, whose "coming out" ball is this? The ball is the scene of the Lodger's "coming out." Not of course, his coming out as a homosexual, for the scene is one of compulsory heterosexuality. Within the narrative of a compulsory heterosexuality always upheld by Hitchcock's narration there is no room for the portrayal of homosexuality other than under the guise of homophobic stereotyping. Instead, what uncontrollably, pathologically, "comes out" is the gentleman's double, the figure of Hyde, or of the Ripper, who murders his sister and women in general because he does not want to "loose" them to (hetero) sexuality and thereby have his own (hetero) sexual impotence exposed.

Jekyll/Ripper and the Virgin/Whore

How does the possibility that the Lodger is Jack the Ripper, consistently entertained by the film, affect our understanding of the film's heroine, Daisy? Ostensibly, as we have seen, Daisy is innocently unaware of the suspicion that the Lodger harbors murderous desires toward her in the scenes I have described, and the film offers a perfectly reasonable explanation of her attraction to the Lodger that is dramatized in the contrast between the Lodger and "average" Joe, between Novello and Malcolm Keen. The difference between them is rather like the difference between Ralph Bellamy and Cary Grant in a later era. Novello, like some American male stars of the silent screen, is graceful, sexually vibrant, and yet sensitive and adoring, in dramatic contrast to Joe, the brutish, sentimental clod. And once the nature of the Lodger's secret is revealed, we are led to understand what it is that makes the Lodger so vibrantly alive. Since he is a man who has stared death in the face, he values life, in particular the life of a young woman like Daisy, above all else. Daisy cannot but be attracted to a man of such sensitivity and caring.

Furthermore, the Lodger is a man that Daisy deserves. Daisy is, in certain respects, the antithesis of the fallen woman. She is a "new woman," a confident agent in the public sphere. Hitchcock's film begins not with the Lodger but with the Lodger's potential victims, who joke about being attacked by a Jack the Ripper figure and cannily disguise their golden curls so as to elude the Ripper's gaze. Daisy herself, a fashion model, is identified with these chorus girls as someone whose control of their self-presentation bestows upon them a sense of agency. Daisy understands the power of the male gaze and is not about to be victimized by it, as her resistance to Joe's blundering advances in the film suggest. Rather than being condemned as an inauthentic expression of identity, Hitchcock's film suggests that the female masquerade is a source of empowerment, that the very source of identity lies in the presentation of self.[43]

Nonetheless, the fact remains that Daisy uses the power of the female masquerade to attract a man who may be a murderer, and while she has blind faith in the innocence of the Lodger, Hitchcock forces us to consider the possibility that a relationship exists between the nascent sexuality of the heroine on the one hand and the proximity in the area of a predatory sexual stalker on the other. Thus while the female masquerade is portrayed as empowering in *The Lodger*, in this way marking the distance of the film from the Victorian mythology of the fallen woman, it remains fraught with ambivalence due to the incipiently lethal character of male (hetero)sexuality. Arguably in expressionistic works such as *The Cabinet of Dr. Caligari* and *Nosferatu*, the self-annihilating force of the virginal heroine's yet-to-be-experienced passion is externally objectified in the uncanny image of the somnambulist, Cesare, and the predatory vampire. In *The Lodger*, the uncanny force of the monster is contained within the figure of the dandy-hero, whose gentlemanly aspect at once suggests and conceals sexual predation. If we take the Lodger to be innocent, then the aura of predation suggests the sense in which, for Hitchcock, predatory and self-annihilating desire is not something that exists in contrast to romance, but rather exists concealed, as a part of romance, immanent but never actualized, fuelling the flames of passion. The actual emergence of this desire would explode the fantasy of romance; its concealment enables romance to take place.[44] On the other hand, if we consider that the Lodger is the Avenger then, Daisy's faith in his innocence suggests something else, a desire to "rescue" the Lodger from his fallen condition and thereby redeem herself.

It is significant in this respect that the young women in *The Lodger* are chorus girls and models, professions that in the Victorian imagination are only one step removed from prostitution. From the standpoint of the Lodger *qua* the Avenger or Jack the Ripper, Daisy is a whore, or at least an incipient whore, if we consider that her relationship to Joe is not yet consummated. His role toward her, like that toward his sister (whom she recalls), is to rescue her from her fallen condition, from her mortality, and to idealize her. By the same token, Daisy's blind faith in the Lodger's innocence resides in the fact that she will rescue him from his fallen condition and absolve herself from her sexuality. She responds to his aversion to women and idealization of her with a maternal love when he "confesses" to her she cradles him in her arms. As a mother figure to the Lodger, Daisy inherits the qualities of Mrs. Bunting in Belloc Lowndes's novel. Thus, if the Lodger is Jekyll/Ripper, Daisy is the Virgin-Mother/Whore. These roles of virgin-mother and whore are entwined as the recto and verso of sexual anxiety, of the fear of/desire for sexual expression that is figured or objectified in Jekyll/Ripper.[45]

Although one risks teleological simplification reading Hitchcock's subsequent films back into his third film, it would be foolish to ignore The Lodger's proleptic status. It introduces many of Hitchcock's enduring obsessions in a strikingly condensed and powerful fashion. As Theodore Price argues, the myth of Jekyll/Ripper and the Virgin/Whore functions as a kind of ur-myth in Hitchcock's film-making career, presumably because its intersections of class and sexual anxieties resonated deeply with Hitchcock's own psychology and background. Hitchcock's successive re-tellings of the myth serve at once to inscribe the legacy of Victorianism in Hitchcock's work and mark out his transformation of that legacy. The Jekyll/Ripper figure functions in the original myth as a source of both fear and fascination, and in both Belloc Lowndes and Hitchcock, Jekyll/Ripper is a source of sympathy.

Hitchcock, following Belloc Lowndes, invites us to respond to the sense of vulnerability in Jekyll/Ripper embodied in Ivor Novello's performance, his fear of being caught out or humiliated, his fear of being shamed, of being seen. In the opening sequence of The Lodger, Hitchcock shoots the back of a newspaper van in such a way that its two oval windows look like eyes and suggest the predatory accusatory eyes of the social order, ready to capture an unwitting victim in their gaze.[46] This motif is repeated, as I have already noted, in the Lodger's room, where two oval portraits stare out at him from the walls like a pair of eyes. Yet Hitchcock's invitation to sympathize with the perpetrator of violence toward woman must be understood in the context of his portrayal of the victim or potential victim. As I have suggested, the original Jekyll/Ripper myth replayed the stereotype of the fallen woman. The Ripper's victims were prostitutes of the lower classes, either to be condemned or saved, but essentially mute victims, and Belloc Lowndes's novel shows sympathy for the female victims only late in the day, as we have seen. However, in Hitchcock's work the idea of the fallen women is inscribed as a symptom rather than a cause of male anxiety, and the portrayal of abjection counterpoised by portrayal of female agency and autonomy.

The Jekyll/Ripper myth combines unspeakable horror and unresolved crime. Since the identity of a criminal lurks beneath the facade of any respectable gentleman and another unspeakable horror remains just around the corner, the myth compels its own retelling. In both the myth of Jekyll/Ripper and its re-telling in *The Lodger*, we find the source of Hitchcock's particular approach to story telling, where the"compulsory" formula of the romance narrative realized on the idealized surfaces of the silver screen is at once relentlessly subverted by masculine heterosexual impotence and incipient violence provoked by strong, sexually independent women, and yet, at the same time, preserved, because for Hitchcock, the Victorian, there is no escape from the double-bind of compulsory heterosexuality other than the pleasures of its staging in the medium of film.

Notes

1. My debt to Ken Mogg's conversation, critical input, and ongoing writing on Hitchcock exceeds my capacity to acknowledge him adequately. My thanks also to Pat McGilligan, Sam Ishii-Gonzalès, and Sid Gottlieb, an ideal editor and collaborator.

2. The passages by W.T. Stead are quoted from Judith Walkowitz, *City of Dreadful Delight: Narratives of Sexual Danger in*

Late-Victorian London (Chicago: University of Chicago Press, 1992), 97-98.

3. Walkowitz, *City of Dreadful Delight*, 206.

4. As Walkowitz notes, "To stabilize and fix Hyde's sexual obsession within the boundaries of heterosexuality . . . the theater version added a new female character, Jekyll's fiancée, murdered by a jealous Hyde, thus injecting heterosexual love and sadism into the closeted professional bachelor world of Jekyll and his friends" (*City of Dreadful Delight*, 206).

5. On this aspect of the fallen woman, see Amanda Anderson, *Tainted Souls and Painted Faces The Rhetoric of Fallenness in Victorian Culture* (Ithaca: Cornell University Press, 1993).

6. Peter Conrad, *The Hitchcock Murders* (London: Faber and Faber, 2000), 67. Jason Rasmussen explores the connection between Wilde and Hitchcock in "Hitchcock, Sexuality, and Self," *The MacGuffin* 24 (1998), 23-28.

7. Sigmund Freud, "Fragment of an Analysis of a Case of Hysteria," *Standard Edition of the Complete Psychological Works of Sigmund Freud*, vol. 7 (London: Hogarth Press and The Institute of Psycho-Analysis, 1953-73), 50.

8. Chasseguet-Smirgel's careful reading of Freud on perversion has been largely ignored by humanities scholars. Most salient in this context is *Creativity and Perversion* (New York: Norton, 1984). See also *The Ego Ideal: A Psychoanalytic Essay on the Malady of the Ideal*, trans. Paul Barrows (New York: Norton, 1985). By invoking Chasseguet-Smirgel as a Freudian, I mean to emphasize the fact that she elaborates a logic implicit in Freud's views, and therefore one that should be understood and assessed historically, alongside and in relationship to Wilde's elaboration of the same themes.

9. See Sigmund Freud "On Narcissism," *Standard Edition*, vol. 14, 73-104. Freud, as far as I am aware, does not discuss the figure of the dandy explicitly. The significance of the figure of the dandy for Hitchcock is broached by Thomas Elsaesser in "The Dandy in Hitchcock," in Richard Allen and S. Ishii-Gonzalès, eds., *Alfred Hitchcock: Centenary Essays* (London: BFI, 1999), 3-13.

10. Hitchcock's complex dramatization of the kiss is explored, though not quite in these terms, by Sidney Gottlieb in "Hitchcock and the Art of the Kiss: A Preliminary Survey," *Hitchcock Annual* (1997-98), 68-86.

11. See François Truffaut, *Hitchcock* (London: Granada Publishing, 1978), 48.

12. Marie Belloc Lowndes, *The Lodger* (Chicago: Academy, 1988), 88.

13. John Ruskin, *Modern Painters*, vol. 5 (New York: Dutton, 1905), 253.

14. In his "After-Dinner Speech at the Screen Producers Guild Dinner" (1965), for example, Hitchcock pointed out that "one of television's greatest contributions is that it brought murder back into the home where it belongs," reprinted in *Hitchcock on Hitchcock: Selected Writings and Interviews*, ed. Sidney Gottlieb (Berkeley: University of California Press, 1995), 58.

15. Belloc Lowndes, *The Lodger*, 38.

16. Although he doesn't detail a history of the use of the term "queer" as meaning "homosexual," Alan Sinfield argues that "the image of the queer" as the effeminate dandy was consolidated after the Wilde trials; see *The Wilde Century: Effeminacy, Oscar Wilde, and the Queer Moment* (New York: Columbia University Press, 1994). George Chauncey claims that homosexuals in New York identified themselves as queer "by the 1910s and 1920s," but in a manner that distinguished them from those who identified themselves as effeminate; see *Gay New York: Gender, Urban Culture, and the Making of the Gay Male World, 1890-1940* (New York: Basic Books, 1995), 15-16.

17. Belloc Lowndes, *The Lodger*, 157.

18. Belloc Lowndes, *The Lodger*, 156.

19. Susan Lowndes, ed., *Diaries and Letters of Marie Belloc Lowndes 1911-1947* (London: Chatto and Windus, 1971), 14.

20. For a detailed discussion of the scene, see Charles Barr, *English Hitchcock* (Moffat: Cameron and Hollis, 1999), 36-38.

21. As Ken Mogg has pointed out to me, Hitchcock's first wrong man narrative is the lost film *The Mountain Eagle* (1926), in which one of the characters, Fear O'God, is wrongly arrested for a crime he did not commit.

22. This is noted by Tom Ryall in *Alfred Hitchcock and the British Cinema* (Urbana: University of Illinois Press, 1986), 25.

23. The expressionist influence on Hitchcock is discussed in Theodore Price, *Hitchcock and Homosexuality: His 50-Year Obsession with Jack The Ripper and the Superbitch Prostitute—A Psychoanalytic View* (Metuchen, NJ.: Scarecrow Press, 1992), 288-354; Sidney Gottlieb, "Early Hitchcock: The German Influence," *Hitchcock Annual* (1999), 100-130; Sarah Street, "*The Lodger*" in Jill Forbes and Sarah Street, eds., *European Cinema* (Basingstoke: Palgrave, 2000), 72-74; and Bettina Rosenblatt in "Shadow of the Immortal Soul:

Hitchcock's *Shadow of a Doubt* and Its Relation to the German Romantic Doppelganger,'' forthcoming in Richard Allen and Sam Ishii-Gonzalès, eds., *Hitchcock: Past and Future* (New York: Routledge, 2002).

24. Donald Rumbelow, *Jack the Ripper: The Complete Casebook* (New York: Contemporary Books, 1988), 165-66. The source for this quotation is given as the *People's Journal*, 26 September 1919, from an article written on the retirement of Detective Steve White.

25. As Patrick McGilligan notes in his forthcoming biography, Hitchcock was an avid reader of police reports during his youth. He may even have read Detective White's report in the *People's Journal* (he was 20 in 1919).

26. See *Close Up* 7, no. 2 (August 1930), 146-47. The exact quote from the interview reads: '' '*Potemkin*,' he continued with a twinkle in his eye, 'is the only Russian film I have seen. Personally, I place a good deal of trust in my feeling for musical formulas.' '' The reference to the musical analogy may suggest the influence of reading Eisenstein, or some of the French theorist-filmmakers of the 1920s whose films were also screened at the London Film Society. I thank Sid Gottlieb for this reference.

27. On British censorship of the film, see James C. Robertson, *The Hidden Cinema: British Film Censorship in Action, 1913-1972* (London: Routledge, 1989), 27-31. My thanks to Casper Tyborg and David Bordwell for alerting me to this chronology and its implications for assessing Eisenstein's possible influence on Hitchcock.

28. On *Potemkin*'s Berlin run, see Richard Taylor, *The Battleship Potemkin* (New York: I.B. Taurus, 2000), 98-122. Production history on *The Lodger* is given by Donald Spoto in *The Dark Side of Genius* (New York: Da Capo Press, 1983), 84-89.

29. See Ivor Montagu, *With Eisenstein in Hollywood* (Berlin: Seven Seas Publishers, 1974), 28-29.

30. By repeating the same action in consecutive shots, the sequence seems to borrow from the bunk lowering sequence in Eisenstein's *Potemkin*, where the same technique was used.

31. Truffaut, *Hitchcock*, 53.

32. William Rothman, *Hitchcock: The Murderous Gaze* (Cambridge: Harvard University Press, 1982), 22. The profile of the Lodger in this scene suggests the Janus-face explored by Brigitte Peucker in ''The Cut of Representation: Painting and Sculpture in Hitchcock,'' in *Alfred Hitchcock: Centenary Essays*, 141-58. Murnau's lost film *Janus-Face* (*Der Januskopf*, 1920) was a retelling of *Dr. Jekyll*

and Mr. Hyde that employed the visual motif of the Janus-face to characterize his "split-personality." See Lotte Eisner, *Murnau* (Berkeley and Los Angeles: University of California Press, 1973), 21.

33. Lesley Brill, *The Hitchcock Romance* (Princeton: Princeton University Press, 1988), 88.

34. Rothman, *Hitchcock: The Murderous Gaze*, 25.

35. Barr, *English Hitchcock*, 41.

36. Lindsay Anderson, "Alfred Hitchcock," in *Focus on Hitchcock*, ed. Albert J. LaValley (Englewood Cliffs NJ: Prentice Hall, 1972), 49.

37. Brill, *The Hitchcock Romance*, 92.

38. See Richard Allen, "Hitchcock, or the Pleasures of Metaskepticism," in *Alfred Hitchcock: Centenary Essays*, 221-37.

39. Rothman, *Hitchcock: The Murderous Gaze*, 46-47; Ken Mogg, "Hitchcock's *The Lodger*: A Theory," *Hitchcock Annual* (1992), 115-127.

40. See Eve Kosofsky Sedgwick, *Between Men: English Literature and Male Homosocial Desire* (New York: Columbia University Press, 1985), 83-117.

41. Sedgwick, *Epistemology of the Closet* (Berkeley: University of California Press, 1990), 205.

42. Quoted in Sedgwick, *Epistemology of the Closet*, 205.

43. On the role of the female masquerade in general, see Joan Rivière, "Womanliness as Masquerade," *International Journal of Psychoanalysis* 10 (1929), 303-313. On the female masquerade in Hitchcock, see Sarah Berry " 'She's Too Everything": Marriage and Masquerade in *Rear Window* and *To Catch a Thief*," in this issue of the *Hitchcock Annual*, 79-107.

44. The role of what I call predatory self-annihilating desire corresponds here to the role of what Slavoj Žižek, after Lacan, calls the real: "The role of the Lacanian real is . . . radically ambiguous: true, it erupts in the form of a traumatic return, derailing the balance of our daily lives, but it serves at the same time as a support of this very balance." See *Looking Awry: An Introduction to Lacan Through Popular Culture* (Cambridge: MIT Press, 1992), 29.

45. On the figure of the Virgin/Whore, see Price *Hitchcock and Homosexuality*, 188. Throughout his book Price emphasizes the thematic complementarity of the figures of Jekyll/Hyde and the Virgin/Whore.

46. Hitchcock discusses this shot in Truffaut, *Hitchcock*, 50-51. The theme it embodies has been articulated persuasively by Žižek as the returned gaze, the look of the object or the world back at the perceiver that renders them vulnerable to exposure or reveals their impotence. See Žižek, "The Hitchcockian Blot," in *Looking Awry*, 88-106.

"SHE'S TOO EVERYTHING": MARRIAGE AND MASQUERADE IN *REAR WINDOW* AND *TO CATCH A THIEF*

SARAH BERRY

Grace Kelly has been said to embody Alfred Hitchcock's ideal of feminine "sexual elegance," the cool blonde who conceals a powerful libido beneath her refined manners.[1] But the characters she plays in both *Rear Window* (1954) and *To Catch a Thief* (1955) are also strong-willed and financially independent women whose self-assurance results in relationship problems. Her autonomy and self-confidence make her "too perfect," threatening her would-be partners and throwing them off balance. While each film ends with its couple on the brink of marriage, there is no serious resolution of these gender conflicts. Instead, the heroine engages in what Joan Rivière, in a 1929 psychoanalytic case study, called a "masquerade of womanliness"—the self-protective use of highly feminine behavior to mask character traits considered masculine, such as intellect or self-confidence.[2] In *Rear Window* Lisa Fremont softens her professional image and possibly gives up her career, while in *To Catch a Thief*, Francie Stevens plays down her assertiveness by turning herself into a seductive fetish object. The effort both women must make to appear non-threatening doesn't dampen their desire to marry the men they love, but simply offers a challenge to their performative skills.

This paper will argue that Kelly's assertive femininity in these films reveals growing cracks in the "separate spheres" marriage of the 1950s, tensions that appear in earlier Hitchcock films and culminate in his later dystopic romances. In *Rear Window* and *To Catch a Thief*, the road to marriage is represented as a struggle for control in which the women find that they must camouflage their equality in order to win a proposal. Marriage thus acts to contain women within traditional norms of femininity, but the note of irony sounded at the end of each film suggests that this accommodation is primarily tactical. As in later films like *Vertigo* (1958), femininity has a double edge, because it represents both the power exerted over women and the power they assume by manipulating their self-presentation in order to elude control. These films suggest that, as performative beings, women can never be truly known and therefore never possessed. This use of feminine appearances as a defensive tactic is perhaps metaphorically alluded to in *Marnie* (1964), when Mark Rutland (Sean Connery) comments, "To escape the eyes of hungry birds, insects disappear in the illusion of a beautiful flower."

Costume is central to Hitchcock's representation of this subversive masquerade, since clothing is used not only to indicate the heroines' shifting "presentation of self," but also to associate femininity with clothing and performance.[3] Hitchcock was particularly interested in the role of costume in his films and paid a great deal of attention to it, particularly the use of color. Designer Edith Head, who worked on eleven of Hitchcock's films (beginning with *Notorious* in 1946), described Hitchcock's involvement in the design process: "Alfred Hitchcock is the only person who works on a script with such detail that a designer could go ahead and make the clothes without discussing them with him."[4] Of Kelly's costumes in *Rear Window* she said that "Every costume was indicated when he sent me the script. There was a reason for every color, every style, and he was absolutely certain about everything he settled on."[5] Hitchcock's postwar films frequently featured Christian Dior's postwar "New Look," which epitomized theatrical femininity with its neo-Victorian cinched waists, full skirts, or long, narrow ones that inhibited walking. *Vogue* magazine commented in 1954 that the style had a "romanticism that bordered closely on "costume.""[6] The silhouette appeared in 1947, as women were being told to quit their wartime jobs and go back to being housewives, and its exaggeration of women's secondary sexual characteristics (breasts and hips) seems designed to reinforce gender difference and traditional social roles. But, as *Vogue* suggested, the nostalgia of the style was also reminiscent of costume drama, which made its femininity seem "put on." Elisabeth Wilson observed that, "although the New Look was supposed to be feminine, there was a weird masculinity about it all. The models were all tall as guardsmen . . . with sharply jutting hips and flying panels which bore faint memories of Gothic architecture."[7] The style was softened somewhat in the 1950s, and its continued popularity was due in large part to the work of Edith Head. She made the silhouette less angular but still emphasized its dynamic qualities by using bouffant skirts and hourglass curves, playing up the ambiguous meanings of its theatrical femininity.

Hitchcock uses the New Look, and costume more generally, both to emphasize the performativity of gender and as an object lesson in the social construction of identity. This is apparent when clothing is used to frame the innocent or disguise the guilty, indicating a desire for clothing to represent a kind of truth that it ultimately cannot. Instead it stands as a social or psychic projection, just as George Kaplan's suit, discovered by Roger Thornhill (Cary Grant) in *North by Northwest*, seems to reveal something about a man who turns out, in fact, not to exist at all. Thornhill's predicament epitomizes the problem of social identity in Hitchcock: once cast in the role of George Kaplan, he can only escape through an even more manipulative use of performance (by faking his own death). Similarly, women in Hitchcock cannot escape femininity; they can only modify their performance of it. Gender roles are thus linked to mistaken identity, performance, and the social forces that define individuals. Susan Smith notes that Hitchcock often emphasizes social performativity to create a "character-istically ironic perspective on deceptiveness of appearances."[8] One context for this is the staging of suspenseful action in the midst of a formal party or social event, using an "out-wardly convivial atmosphere as a screen for the playing-out of much more private, much less sociable feelings."[9] This paper will suggest that marriage is another context in which inner power struggles are masked by conventional behavior, highlighting the increasing fragility of traditional gender roles in the postwar context. Hitchcock's heroines use performance as a defensive strategy, suffering what Richard Millington, describing Eve Kendall (Eva Marie Saint) in *North by Northwest*, calls "the double consciousness" of her existence as both a person and a "commodity" of exchange between male government agents.[10] Hitchcock's women are thus inured to the process of consciously performing and modulating their identities as a tactical necessity, while men become aware of the fragility of their social identity only once it is threatened.

Hitchcock and Marriage:
From Male Domination to Feminine Dissimulation

Hitchcock's postwar films focus on marriage and gender roles to a greater degree than his earlier work, but his representation of marriage as fraught with conflict extends back to earlier films as well. Paula Marantz Cohen has suggested that Hitchcock's films of the 1940s and 1950s are his most "character centered," as a result of both producer David O. Selznick's commercial interest in the "woman's picture" and Hitchcock's own Victorian upbringing.[11] But they are also those in which the couple often represents a source of deep psychological tension within the films, which remains unresolved by romantic closure. Cohen and others have also pointed out that Hitchcock's work from this period, particularly with James Stewart, emphasizes the postwar crisis in American masculinity by rendering male characters with greater attention to their emotional subjectivity.[12] What has received less comment is that these films also feature heroines faced with a crisis around gender roles because of the apparent conflict between marriage and their own desires to define themselves or who have a career—feelings that are not resolved at the end of the films. As Cohen points out, Hitchcock's films from the late 1950s onward seem to abandon all hope for the traditional couple, and instead voice the confusion and loss of a patriarchal culture "no longer secure in a stable, gender-differentiated identity." But she sees this as a break with his earlier work:

> Hitchcock's drive of the 1940s and 1950s had been the attempt to reclaim novelistic (i.e., psychological) character for cinematic representation and to accommodate gender complementarity to this reclamation process. *Rear Window* had been about the construction of subjectivity for its male protagonist, while *The Man Who Knew Too Much* meshed the gender characteristics of the couple.[13]

I would like to suggest that there is, instead, a strong continuity between the highly dystopic romances explored in later films such as *Vertigo* (1957), *The Birds* (1963), and *Marnie* (1964), and the problematic couple formation seen earlier in Hitchcock's work throughout the 1940s and 1950s, particularly in postwar films such as *Rear Window* and *To Catch a Thief*.

The theme of marriage as the male domination of a woman appears early on in Hitchcock's female gothic-influenced films, but by the late 1950s and 1960s, Hitchcock's pessimism about gender relations is quite pronounced, culminating in what Michele Piso calls Hitchcock's "trilogy of modern despair": *Psycho* (1960), *The Birds*, and *Marnie*.[14] *Marnie* is a particularly direct exploration of the complex power struggles manifested in marriage, and one that casts a revealing light on earlier couples such as those in *Rear Window* and *To Catch a Thief*. The heroine, Marnie Edgar (Tippi Hedren), is a compulsive thief whose latest crime is discovered by Mark Rutland (Sean Connery), a wealthy man who is attracted to her transgressive behavior. Marnie has previously eluded capture by taking on multiple identities and transforming herself through dress, hair color, and performance. Mark offers her a choice between prison and marriage, convinced that he can "help" Marnie by stripping away her false identities and confronting her with the childhood trauma that has led her to become a thief. Having

taken her as his wife, however, he literally strips her of
clothing and forces her to have sex against her will, resulting
in her attempted suicide. Mark's desire to possess the "real"
Marnie is, like Scottie's (James Stewart) compulsion to
recreate and possess Madeleine (Kim Novak) in *Vertigo*, just
as neurotic as Marnie's own behavior (a point she makes in
the film). Piso thus rejects the "therapeutic" reading of
Marnie, according to which Marnie is healed by the confrontation with her past and able to move from her thwarted
desire for a mother's love to the protective arms of a man.[15]
Piso argues instead that Mark sees marriage "not as integration but domination":

> So accustomed is he to owning, so synonymous is his
> sexuality with social power, that he assumes he can
> possess Marnie too, violate her, break her down, and
> then build her back up (in his image, his language, in
> the image of the "normal" female).[16]

What Hitchcock seems at pains to point out in *Marnie* is that
the "normal" identity Mark wants her to take up is no more
real and no less performative than her own life of independent subterfuge. Following their marriage, he directs Marnie
in her new role: "This is a drill, dear. Wife follows husband
to door, gives and/or gets a kiss, stands pensively as he
drives away. A wistful little wave is optional."

The remainder of this essay will look at *Rear Window* and
To Catch a Thief in light of the questions about marriage,
gender, and performance raised explicitly in *Marnie* and
indirectly in much of Hitchcock's work—questions about
whether marriage can accommodate equal partners and whether
gender roles can be redefined to acknowledge women's
equality. *Marnie* ends with the issue of marriage ominously
unresolved, as Marnie asks, "Will I have to go to jail? I'd
rather stay with you," and Mark replies with the lingering
question, "Had you, love?" Similarly, *Rear Window* and *To
Catch a Thief* both conclude on the brink of a marriage
proposal, but also with an ironic gesture or comment

suggesting a tenuous truce in an unresolved battle of the sexes. This indeterminacy is in part because the heroine's "masquerade of womanliness" presents a paradox for the men in these films. It represents both the containment of women within patriarchal conventions and, at the same time, the ambiguity of their submission, since the "real" woman may remain unattainable or covertly resistive.

Rear Window:
"Are You Real, Mona Lisa?"

In *Rear Window* the theme of marriage and feminine subterfuge is treated with more irony and humor than in *Marnie*, focusing on the problems of a two-career couple. Lisa Fremont (Grace Kelly) and L.B. Jefferies (James Stewart) are both independent and career-minded, a situation that, for Jeff, makes marriage impossible. Lisa seeks compromise, while Jeff rebuffs her but refuses to end the relationship. As with *Marnie*, a common reading of the film is as a "therapeutic" narrative. According to Robin Wood, for example, Lisa and Jeff both become more amenable to the other's position and by the end are ready to form a companionate marriage. By uncovering Mrs. Thorwald's murder, Jeff repudiates his fearful identification with Lars Thorwald (Raymond Burr): "his desire to be rid of [Lisa] is abruptly given a form so direct as to be unacceptable: dream has become nightmare."[17] Lisa, conversely, is said to go from a concern with "passive" self-display to a more "active" participation in Jeff's murder mystery, making her more compatible with his lifestyle. But Lisa is initially very actively involved in her *own* career, and as Elise Lemire has suggested, her movement is not one from passive to active, but from public to private:

> If Jeff doesn't want to marry Lisa, it is because her job keeps her in the public sphere, the sphere in which he rightfully belongs but from which he has been banned. His fear of her sexuality could certainly be a symptom of this larger issue.[18]

While Jeff is, as Tania Modleski points out, "feminized" by his confinement with a broken leg and temporarily put in the female Gothic heroine's position of entrapment and vulnerability in the home, this does not result in his rejection of male dominance.[19] Instead of gaining respect for Lisa's public life and autonomy, Jeff insists that she accept his point of view and version of events. As John Belton argues,

> Lisa's self-display is an attempt to control [Jeff's] gaze. Jeff, however, resists her strategy and tries, instead, to force Lisa to abandon her own attempts to control his gaze and to submit herself to his gaze, to join him in his voyeuristic activities. In other words . . . he wants to dominate her.[20]

Jeff becomes willing to marry Lisa only once she stops talking about her own work, starts to share his view of events ("tell me everything you saw, and what you think it means"), enters his domestic space ("I'll trade you my feminine intuition for a room for the night"), and becomes his helpmate. Jeff also stops fearing marriage as a form of male imprisonment once he enters the domestic sphere himself and finds it a far more dangerous environment for women. Modleski notes this association of marriage with women's vulnerability in the context of the climactic shot of Lisa in Thorwald's apartment with Anna Thorwald's ring on her finger. While François Truffaut, in his interview with Hitchcock, admired this moment as a "double victory" for Lisa—she wears the ring that will both solve the case and make Jeff want to marry *her*—Modleski points out that it is the ring of a dead woman: "Just as Miss Lonelyhearts . . . has gone looking for a little companionship and romance and ended up nearly being raped, so Lisa's ardent desire for marriage leads straight to a symbolic wedding with a wife-murderer."[21]

Initially, Jeff sees marriage as a form of male entrapment. (Stella [Thelma Ritter] says that someday Miss Lonelyhearts will find her happiness, to which Jeff replies, "Yes, and some man will lose his.") But by the end of the film he lies smiling under Lisa's proprietary gaze, indicating that he has become reconciled to their marriage. What, exactly, has changed Jeff's mind? One possibility is that Lisa's bravery in climbing into Thorwald's apartment makes Jeff realize that she is, after all, capable of being the wife of an adventurous photojournalist. There are two other developments, however, that are equally significant. One is that Jeff becomes deeply engrossed in the daily life of his neighbors and becomes aware of its undercurrent of domestic violence against women. Rather than continuing to see marriage as a form of male entrapment, it is possible that some of Jeff's fear is allayed by the discovery that marriage tends to disempower women rather than men. The second significant change is in Lisa's self-presentation to Jeff, which moves from glamorous power-dressing to a softer, more vulnerable look associated with sexuality and, in the final scenes, with nature. Her behavior and discourse also change quite dramatically, as she stops telling Jeff about her work and instead begins to mirror his own preoccupations. In the following analysis of the film I will emphasize these changes in both Jeff's perspective on marriage and in Lisa's self-image. As I suggested earlier, the film ends ambiguously because, while Jeff now sees wifehood as a form of containment, the viewer is well aware that it may also be a masquerade, which Lisa indicates when she surreptitiously reads the fashion magazine that symbolizes her own career.

Jeff introduces the problem of his incompatibility with Lisa by complaining to his nurse Stella that Lisa is "too talented, too beautiful, too sophisticated—she's too everything but what I want." Lisa's femininity clearly carries a disturbing amount of social power, which is highlighted by her first appearance in the film. While Jeff sleeps she appears as a dark shadow cast across his face. A reverse angle shot shows Kelly's "perfect" visage looking adoringly at him. Jeff's eyes flutter open and he looks perturbed as he glances up to see her. Slowly his expression changes from one of vague apprehension to a tepid smile as she leans down to kiss him in a point-of-view shot filled with her shiny red lips and looming face. In spite of her glamorous appearance, the somewhat menacing shadow she casts and Jeff's lackluster response to her kiss reflect his ambivalence about their relationship.[22] When Jeff responds with the question, "Who are you?" she proceeds to introduce herself as though on stage, lighting herself dramatically and striking a pose to show off her new dress. He quips, "Oh, you mean the Lisa Fremont who never wears the same dress twice?" She responds, "Only because it's expected of me." This is one of Jeff's many digs at her line of work, but it also voices anxiety about women's ability to transform themselves with clothing and thus be continually elusive. The "femininity-as-performance" theme is underscored later in the same scene when Jeff sees Miss Lonelyhearts preparing for an imaginary guest—her coquettish greeting at the door is, like Miss Torso's seductive dancing, an exaggerated rehearsal of femininity for an absent male audience.

Lisa's visual dominance in Jeff's apartment is emphasized through color. In the opening sequence when the camera pans slowly around Jeff's room to show the signs of his occupation and accident, Jeff wears brown pajamas and the walls and décor are uniformly brown and beige. When Lisa enters, she stands out dramatically in her red lipstick, blue eye shadow, and black-and-white gown. The dress is a modified version of the New Look, with a very full white skirt and fitted black V-necked bodice, cut elegantly to each shoulder. Other than black embroidery below the waistline, it is unembellished, and she wears a simple pearl necklace, bracelet, and tulle shawl. The usual push-up-bra femininity of the New Look is tempered by the modesty of the bodice: instead of emphasizing Lisa's bust with a corset-like, strapless neckline (as worn by Miss Torso in this scene), it is demurely sophisticated. The frothy skirt sways around her like sea foam when she moves, and when the red-jacketed waiter from "21" enters the room it becomes animated with color and movement. Jeff, by contrast, is visually associated with dead colors and immobility, which is ironic given his claim, during their argument, that he can't marry Lisa because she could never keep up with his active lifestyle. Jeff's pajamas change color from brown to light blue after this scene, however, which keeps him in a generically masculine color (later contrasted with Lisa's pale pink negligee) but also brings him into the softer color palette that will mark the transition in Lisa's image. The couple gradually becomes more visually compatible, but traditional gender distinctions are maintained, marked by their pink and blue costumes.

The femininity of Lisa's gown is modified in several interesting ways, particularly by comparison with her later costumes. It is black and white, as is the dress worn in her second scene, which is black and worn with pearls. She describes the first dress as work clothing, mentioning its price and asking Jeff if he thinks it will sell. It is thus, like the black and white of a man's suit, her business attire, and she reinforces this by talking animatedly about her busy schedule at work that day. In Lisa's second scene, the camera pans across the courtyard and finds her kissing Jeff, who is distracted. Lisa is again in black, and this time the dress has a stiffer, accordion-pleated skirt of transparent fabric over an opaque lining with a shiny black belt. The shawl collar and short sleeves are of the transparent black fabric, which is twisted across the bust over an opaque, fitted bodice. It looks slightly constraining, with the pleats adding a brittle edge, perhaps reflecting her anger at Jeff. After another day at work Lisa only wants Jeff's sexual attention and becomes extremely annoyed at his disinterest in her and preoccupation with the neighbors. This is a reversal of the typical roles in which a husband returns home expecting his wife's attention, uninterested in her domestic social world. Lisa also becomes physically dominant, as she yanks his wheelchair from the window, takes away his binoculars, and leans over him while gripping the arms of his chair. The business-like quality of Lisa's first two dresses also contrasts with the women across the courtyard: Miss Lonelyhearts wears a faded green dress that matches her green couch and contrasts with her sadly un-cheerful pink walls. Miss Torso wears a New Look strapless dress while serving drinks to three men. It accentuates her figure but is made of a metallic silver fabric, illustrating the two ways of reading her behavior offered by Jeff and Lisa: either she is seducing the men with her low-cut dress, or she is fending off the "wolves" in her armor-like, metallic dress. In both cases these women offer a clear contrast with Lisa's sophisticated power dressing.

Jeff's perspective changes significantly between the initial fight with Lisa and her next visit. The film also changes its tone at this point, from that of a lighthearted drama about a two-career couple to a film noir-like vision of the dark undercurrents beneath a seemingly innocent community of neighbors. This change occurs after the fight when Lisa leaves the apartment angrily; Jeff looks out at the courtyard, which is now cast in a dark blue light, and the sounds of the street become loud. The camera pans over to the Song-writer's dark window, and then jerks suddenly up to the corner apartment where a couple with a young daughter were shown in the opening scene. A remarkable moment follows, which has received almost no comment in dis-cussions of the film: there is the sound of broken glass and a woman's piercing scream, followed by the cry, "Don't!" Jeff reacts to these sounds of domestic violence with an alarmed expression—his eyes dart around to each of his neighbors' windows, as though he now suspects that this is a different social space than the one he jokingly spied on during the day.

After this mood transition, Jeff spends a sleepless night watching the courtyard and becoming increasingly suspicious about Thorwald's actions. This night sequence marks a change in Jeff's attitude to his female neighbors, which shows an increasing awareness of their isolation in the home. In the opening scene, Jeff's voyeurism is represented as typically male—while on the phone with his editor he ogles Miss Torso and two girls sunbathing on their roof while a helicopter hovers overhead, echoing Jeff's own behavior. After the night scene, however, Jeff's attitude is different, as he tells Stella that Miss Lonelyhearts "drank herself to sleep again last night" and comments that Thorwald may be leaving his wife. Jeff begins to perceive his female neighbors as vulnerable in a way that was entirely absent from his initial, objectifying comments. But if Jeff's entry into the world of domesticity and neighborhood gossip gives him a more feminine perspective, it certainly doesn't turn him into a feminist. He continues to be dismissive of Lisa's career and annoyed by her sexual advances, as though his forced passivity makes her vitality even more of a threat. Adding to his annoyance is the fact that Lisa takes a traditionally masculine attitude towards his interest in the neighbors. Her initially skeptical attitude is later voiced by Lt. Doyle, while Lisa instead takes up Jeff's point of view, bringing herself, Stella, and Jeff together in the feminine discourse of intuition and gossip and leaving Lt. Doyle to represent masculine, rational disinterest. Lisa's move from a masculine to a feminine position is indicated when, following the night that she accepts Jeff's story, she arrives at the apartment looking much softer and more vulnerable. She wears an elegant pale green suit with a white pillbox hat and short veil, white gloves, and a girlish pearl charm bracelet. The color of her suit is quite significant, since in *Rear Window* green is primarily associated with Miss Lonelyhearts, who wears first a faded green dress, then a deep green one when she goes out (only to be assaulted), and finally a blue-green dressing gown for her planned suicide. Pale green was one of Hitchcock's favorite colors for women, but he also used it, as with Miss Lonelyhearts, in association with vulnerability and death.

Lisa's image also changes because she immediately begins removing her clothing, a process that ends with her in a negligée that is, as John Fawell notes, "a dead ringer for the one we have seen, from a distance, the murder victim, Mrs. Thorwald wear." Fawell suggests that "the specter of the murdered wife offers a macabre undercurrent" to Lisa's most sexual appearance, emphasizing the sadism of Jeff's desire to dominate her.[23] I would argue that Jeff's temporarily femininized position changes his image of Mrs. Thorwald from a negative one of power (the henpecking wife who drives her husband to murder) to a less threatening one (the invalid wife abandoned for another woman). Lisa's new appearance—stripped of her work identity, safely ensconced in the home, and mirroring a woman who has been killed by her husband—is desirable to Jeff because she is beginning to conform to his new sense of women's disempowerment by marriage.

Lisa's offer to Jeff of her "feminine intuition" for a place to sleep also presents marriage as a kind of exchange, suggesting a relationship between marriage and money that is also played out when Lars Thorwald is seen digging through his dead wife's jewelry. As I will argue in relation to *To Catch a Thief*, Hitchcock's men often equate women's bodies and money, seeing both as their rightful possessions (in *Psycho*, Marion imagines her boss discovering the stolen money and exclaiming, "I'll get it back, and if any of it's missing I'll replace it with her fine, soft, flesh!"). The clearest articulation of this theme occurs in *Marnie*, in which Marnie finds out that she was conceived because a boy offered her mother, who later became a prostitute, a sweater for having sex with him. Mrs. Edgar says she agreed because she had "never had anything of her own." Marnie accepts her own marriage only in exchange for her freedom from prison, but this exchange also requires her to have sex with Mark, associating their marriage with her mother's prostitution.[24] Mark, it is worth noting, inherited his money from his dead first wife, which puts him in the company of a number of Hitchcock men who marry women with the expectation of inheriting their money (as in *Suspicion*, *Shadow of a Doubt*, and *Dial M for Murder*). Thorwald's inventory of Anna's jewelry emphasizes this relationship between marriage and male acquisition. Lisa's own handbag prefigures her potential loss of financial autonomy in marriage: in her first scene, she casually pulled enough cash out of her purse to pay for an expensive dinner and the waiter's cab ride. In the scene where she spends the night, her black handbag contains nothing but a sexy negligee and some slippers. Later on, when she has been taken in by the police and Jeff and Stella search for bail money, her purse has only fifty cents in it, underscoring her transition from a threatening career woman to a dependent wife.[25]

As the camera makes its final trip across *Rear Window*'s courtyard, the newlyweds are now fighting: the bride says, "If I'd known you'd lost your job I wouldn't have married you," suggesting both the brevity of the honeymoon phase of their relationship and the tensions caused by women's economic dependence. We are presented with the image of Jeff, now with two broken legs, smiling in spite of his continued immobility. Lisa, significantly, is now wearing blue pants and reading a book about travel adventure. One could conclude that Jeff has finally consented to marry Lisa because she has proven herself to be an adequately adventurous partner. The fact that Lisa is wearing pants would then indicate that she has moved from a preoccupation with feminine self-display to a more masculine and active role. But it is important to note that Lisa's outfit is not simply coded as active and outdoorsy, it is also distinctly casual—pants were worn by women in the 1950s primarily as leisure-wear. Not only has her style changed from indoor to outdoor clothing, then, but also from professional to casual clothing. She also wears a pink blouse, which modifies the masculinity of her outfit and confirms the transition in the palette of her wardrobe from black and white to softer, more feminine colors such as the pink negligée she changed into when spending the night at Jeff's.

Lisa's final costume and the book she reads thus suggest that she may be willing to give up her own career in order to marry Jeff and travel with him. Jeff's smile indicates that he no longer fears being domesticated by Lisa because she has indicated her willingness to adapt to his notion of the ideal wife—one who mirrors him rather than maintaining her own interests. If this marriage looks like a traditional one of female containment, however, Lisa's final gesture of surreptitiously picking up her copy of *Harper's Bazaar* brings that notion into question. As a sign of her own career and lifestyle, the fashion magazine suggests that her new outfit as the outdoorsy wife is part of a conscious but perhaps temporary strategy for winning Jeff's proposal. The irony of the film's romantic resolution thus highlights the paradox of femininity: Lisa has made it clear that her self-presentation is primarily guided by "what's expected" of her, but Jeff wants to see her accommodation as real. The viewer, on the other hand, may notice Lisa's sly glance at Jeff as she picks up the fashion magazine. Hitchcock once again points out that women may be restricted by norms of feminine behavior but they can also manipulate them, playing multiple roles in order to evade control.

To Catch a Thief:
Diamonds are a Man's Best Friend

The problems of modern marriage are treated more cynically in Hitchcock's next film, in which the relationship between Francie Stevens (Grace Kelly) and John Robie (Cary Grant) is marked not only by power struggles, but also the mutual objectification associated with consumer culture. As has been said of *Marnie*, one can argue that in *To Catch a Thief* "all relationships are characterized by cash."[26] Jewelry functions overtly as a fetish object in the film—a substitute for the body that heightens desire—and also symbolizes wealth and conspicuous consumption, both of which are satirized gleefully. The protagonists are treated with great irony and distance, and there is a noticeable lack of intimate close-ups and portrayal of interiority in the treatment of Francie compared to that of the heroines in most of Hitchcock's American films. Francie and John are presented as two of a kind: nouveau riche American consumers who feel entitled to everything they want. The style of the film was clearly influenced by the economics of Hollywood in the 1950s, using its stars, wide-screen VistaVision, locations, color, and costumes as production values. It is a movie about materialism, surface appearances, and people who are not what they seem, and the familiar themes of role playing and false identity are inflected by social satire. Unlike the protagonists of Hitchcock's more "character-centered" films, Francie and John seem to represent social types rather than displaying the "depth psychology" of realist drama. John is an ex-jewel thief ("the Cat") who pretends to be Conrad Burns, an Oregon timber baron, in order to hunt down an imitator who is casting suspicion on him. Francie realizes he is actually the former Cat and assumes he has gone back to a life of crime, which makes him all the more alluring to her.

Like Lisa Fremont, Francie actively pursues her man at first, but he is put off by her advances and refuses to acknowledge that she is correct about his identity as the Cat. Francie responds by switching to a more indirect approach; she associates herself with his object of desire, which is jewelry. Although she succeeds in seducing him, he continues to maintain his own masquerade and refuses to accept her help in finding the real thief. This leads Francie to assume his guilt and presents a roadblock to the romance until Francie's mother (Jesse Royce Landis) finally tells her the truth. In the end, John accepts Francie's help, and they plan an elaborate trap and succeed in catching the real thief. While it is initially unclear why John refuses to confide in Francie, one explanation is that he is well aware that Francie is attracted to his presumed criminality. This is a common trait of both men and women in Hitchcock films (Mark Rutland's interest in *Marnie*, for example), and represents a desire for transgressive sexuality, or as John calls it, "weird excitement." When asked in an interview if Francie would prefer it if John were really the thief, Hitchcock answered, "Oh, of course . . . it's more in the nature of her fetish."[27] *To Catch a Thief* is thus not simply about feminine masquerade and the subversion of marriage, but about a broader topic: the desire for transgressive or elusive objects, which leads people to objectify themselves in order to become more desirable. Men still dominate this libidinal and social economy, however, and Francie's image must shift from that of an active, desiring subject to that of a desirable object waiting to be chosen.

Social relations in general are presented as highly commodified, with the English insurance agent Hughson (John

Williams) and the pesky French ex-Resistance members offering a minor contrast to the film's emphasis on the opulent self-indulgence of the rich. Women's bodies are associated with jewelry, money, and other objects throughout the film, and Francie claims that, in her experience, "money handles most people." Both she and her mother make continual references to buying people and sex, indicating that consumerist objectification cuts across genders. What makes the film's romance particularly ironic is that although Francie gains a proposal from John by making herself appear less threatening (her fetishized body masks the assertiveness of her personality), it is clear that their relationship is based not on mutual understanding but on mutual objectification. Francie wants John because she thinks being a former thief is sexy, and he wants her because she's loaded with money.

Their self-objectification is linked to a theme of social performance that runs through the film, as it does in later films such as *Vertigo* and *North by Northwest*. With the final capture of the thief, Danielle (Brigitte Auber), John demands, "All right, you've got a full house down there, now begin the performance." She asks, "What performance?" and he responds, "You know, the one in which you tell them what is what and who is really who." Calling attention to the usual exposition of crime details at the end of a mystery film adds an element of reflexivity, also seen earlier in Francie's comment on John's somewhat inept masquerade (and perhaps on Cary Grant's star persona):

> You're just not convincing, John. You're like an American character in an English movie. You just don't talk the way an American tourist ought to talk . . . you never mention business or baseball or television or wage freezes or senate probes . . . you're just not American enough to carry it off.

Francie's attitude towards identity and self-presentation is playful and self-consciously theatrical, as she takes on a series of different looks designed to break down John's resistance (the sultry ice-maiden, the "Cat's new kitten," the diamond-laden heiress, and finally, the gold-wrapped bauble he takes home with him). Her masquerade is aimed at bringing the couple together, while his works to keep her at a distance and allow him to remain in control.

The roles of both John and Francie draw on the pre-existing star personae of Cary Grant and Grace Kelly. Although this was only Kelly's sixth starring role on film, her public image as a "cool beauty" with unsuspected reserves of passion was already familiar to American audiences, particularly after her appearance in *Rear Window*.[28] Hitchcock has said that, in order to emphasize Francie's aloof glamour in her first scene, "I deliberately photographed Grace Kelly ice-cold and I kept cutting to her profile, looking classical, beautiful, and very distant."[29] She also wears an icy-blue gown with thin rhinestone straps and a matching transparent blue shawl draped from one shoulder in a familiar fashion trope of "classical" beauty. Having evoked Kelly's refined image, Hitchcock then had her unexpectedly kiss John in the corridor (he later commented, "It's as though she'd unzipped his fly"), highlighting the performativity of her ladylike façade.[30] The role of John Robie was well-suited to Cary Grant's star image, since Grant epitomized the smooth veneer of glamour at a time when method acting was changing the look of masculinity on screen. Hitchcock liked to use Grant's own image as part of his characterizations, commenting, "One doesn't direct Cary Grant, one simply puts him in front of a camera. And, you see, he enables the audience to identify with the main character. I mean that, Cary Grant represents a man we know."[31]

This use of Grant's persona is particularly evident after John finally gives up his disguise as Conrad Burns. Taking off the self-consciously continental suit with an open shirt collar and ascot tie, John's return to "realness" is signified by his appearance as Cary Grant—in one of Grant's iconically familiar pale blue-grey bespoke suits (he preferred to wear his own suits on screen when possible).[32] The dominance of

Grant's star persona heightens the performativity of John's character. Like Johnny Aysgarth in *Suspicion* or Roger Thornhill in *North by Northwest*, John is also presented as someone who lacks "character," which requires a sense of ethics. This becomes clear during John's lunch conversation with Hughson, when John claims that his jewelry thefts were no different than Hughson's cheating on his expense account. His comparison is made all the more absurd by the fact that we have recently heard Danielle tell him, "I was just thinking about you, imagining you in your expensive villa enjoying life while we work like idiots for a loaf of bread." John is presented as an amoral, self-interested person, who cautions Hughson, "You can't do things the honest way in this business—remember that." The emphasis on star performances in the film underscores its focus on the artifice of social behavior, particularly among wealthy consumers who can afford to reinvent themselves by wearing and owning whatever they like. John, for example, has gone from being a circus performer to being one of the beautiful people simply by stealing the means to buy a whole new identity.

Just as the roles of Francie and John are inflected by the theatricality of the actors' pre-existing star personae, the costumes in *To Catch a Thief* draw attention to the performance of identity and are designed for maximum spectacle-value. In addition to their theatricality, however, women's costumes in the film also tend to associate their bodies with other objects in the environment. The film has a color palette dominated by pinks and reds, first seen on the terrace of John's hilltop villa, which is dotted with pink and red flowers. This color scheme later fills the entire VistaVision frame during the flower-market chase, which includes numerous women in pink dresses. The women blend in with the baskets of flowers and, like them, become decorative elements. Similarly, during the film's climactic fancy-dress ball, women move toward the frame of the camera until they are only visible from the neck down, as faceless models for the elaborate necklaces and gowns they wear. This "elaborately vulgar" costume-ball was staged with the sole purpose, according to Edith Head, of displaying Francie in an extravagant gold lamé gown.[33] This is quite revealing, given that Francie is still wearing the gold ball-gown in the film's final scene, in which the couple is united. This illustrates the fact that, while she has finally caught her thief, he has taken possession of her as an embodied piece of jewelry.

Francie's first appearance, as she sits on the beach eyeing John's red swimming trunks, is in a yellow strapless bathing suit with a mini-skirt, a yellow scarf covering her hair, and white sunglasses. She appears in yellow and white several times, next seen the morning after her first dinner with John. The yellow offers a warm contrast with the cool blue dress she is first seen in, particularly since bright yellow light is used throughout the film to indicate the sunny environment. But it also signals her association with money and gradual self-transformation into the gold-wrapped package she becomes in the final scene at the costume ball.

Francie's fourth outfit is particularly eye-catching: having invited John to go swimming, she appears in the hotel lobby dressed in a black body suit topped by white accessories, suggesting that she is ready to shed the accessories and join John's roof-climbing as the Cat-woman. Like Hitchcock's substitution of Marion Crane's white underwear with black in *Psycho* to indicate that she has become a "bad girl," the dramatic black and white geometry of Francie's outfit (she looks like an upside-down exclamation point) may also indicate her moral contradictions: she wants to play at being a thief and seduce one, but when her mother's jewels are finally stolen she is outraged. The style of wearing tight Capri pants with a back panel or full skirt open at the front was a very popular variation on the New Look in the early 1950s, and it is fascinating for the way it offers the mobility of pants while maintaining a feminine silhouette. The skirt-over-pants look is provocative as well as demure, partly exposing and freeing the legs while maintaining a neo-Victorian silhouette—it suggests the use of femininity as a "cover" for more assertive behavior.

Francie's Cat-woman outfit also draws a parallel between her and Danielle, although Danielle's black cat-burglar clothing, unlike Francie's, makes her look both boyish and inconspicuous. Francie's costume, on the other hand, is designed to get attention (several tourists in the hotel lobby gawk at it). But the two women are similar in their aggressive pursuit of John, and in their willingness to describe themselves as objects in order to appeal to his acquisitive nature. In the swimming scene, Danielle asks John ''What has she got more than me, except money—and you are getting plenty of that.'' He replies that Danielle is a girl and Francie is a woman. Danielle responds by comparing herself to a commodity: ''Why would you want to buy an old car when you can get a new one cheaper? It will run better and last longer.'' Similarly, John goes on to describe women as commodities after Danielle says, ''Marvelous . . . last night you steal a small fortune and today you lie on the beach with an American beauty.'' He replies, ''That's why one needs a small fortune.'' In spite of the women's aggressive ''cat fight'' over John in this scene, it is important to note that by the end of the film both women have been punished for their assertiveness: John slaps Danielle across the face at her father's funeral—even before he knows she is the real thief— and sternly rejects Francie, accusing her of insincerity. His angry scolding of Francie is quite jarring, since he has been at least as dishonest with her as she with him. The irony of his moral high-handedness is that both women are behaving exactly like him: Danielle is a jewel thief and Francie is playing a role to get what she wants. The moral superiority John assumes at the end of the film suggests that, although he is no less duplicitous than they, he believes in his own entitlement to define and condemn both women. He also sees the social mobility, wealth, and freedom he has acquired through his own masquerade as legitimate, while Danielle and Francie's dissimulation and self-interest are not. Just as he feels that he is entitled to his stolen goods but Danielle isn't, he seems to think that he can acquire Francie but she must not be allowed to think that she has acquired him.

Following the swimming scene, Francie's next courtship strategy is to use her diamond necklace as bait to seduce John, just as he is using her mother as bait to catch the real thief. She wears a strapless white gown, draped and fitted across the front to emphasize her breasts, which she implicitly refers to while describing her diamonds in a close up of her neck and cleavage: "Look! Hold them! . . . Diamonds—the only thing in the world you can't resist." She asks how he feels being so close to her and unable to possess the jewels. Her movements and gestures are highly stylized, like those of a stage actor, as she describes his scenario of frustration and offers herself as its solution. She steps backward out of the light so that her face is in shadow and she is only visible from the neck down, the sparkling diamonds replacing her face and becoming a substitute for her body itself. He responds, "these diamonds are fake and you know it," to which she replies, "Well I'm not." The irony here is that she *is* being fake—her words are entirely contradicted by her mannered behavior and the fact that they are both manipulating one another: he still pretends not to be Robie and she still plays at being his accomplice. The parodic intercutting of the fireworks places quotation marks around the whole scene and underscores the artifice of their personalities and sexual relationship. In comparing her body to the necklace, Francie adds to the film's discourse about buying people or sex. This scene also suggests that, while Francie willingly objectifies herself to attract John, he is more interested in her money than her body. Their previous love scenes are decidedly passionless, and after showing off her "diamonds" she practically has to drag John onto the couch.

If *To Catch a Thief* suggests that marriage, for both Francie and John, is a form of acquisition, it does so in the context of a culture obsessed with material acquisition. This commodification of social relations does not, however, level the playing field in terms of either class or gender. Although the film suggests that all wealth is more or less illegitimate (Mrs. Stevens admits that Francie's father was a ''swindler''), John has ended up in the social elite (perched high on a hill) while his former Resistance comrades work in the basement of a restaurant. Similarly, there is a notably gendered power differential between John, on one hand, and Danielle and Francie on the other. John's behavior is no less immoral or selfish than that of Danielle and Francie, but he punishes Francie by claiming she has wronged him, and aligns himself with the Law in order to punish Danielle. This gendered power difference can also be seen in John's accusation that Francie treats people like playthings, since he becomes more responsive to her after she stops asking to become his partner and begins presenting herself to him as a thing. His double standard is made particularly clear to the viewer, because his condemnation of Francie comes immediately following a scene in which he has a jocular exchange with Bertani about the benefits of marrying Francie for her money, thus reducing her to a valuable object of exchange. In the end, Francie continues to chase John but presents herself not as his accomplice, but as his helpmate (she asks him to admit that he couldn't have caught the thief without the "help of a good woman"). She becomes increasingly pliant and contrite, and her more traditionally feminine demeanor encourages him to feel that he has successfully tamed this "headstrong girl." As with Lisa in *Rear Window*, however, Francie has the last word, which indicates that her subordinate attitude may be a ruse. After she and John embrace, she looks around his home and says, "Oh, mother will love this." By verbally taking possession of his villa and installing her mother in it, Francie reverts to her original sense of entitlement and indicates that her submissiveness may be tactical rather than real.

Conclusion

In one of his earliest films, *The Lodger* (1926), Hitchcock introduced a recurring theme of marriage as the capture of a woman by a man. The heroine of the film is courted by a policeman, who playfully handcuffs her to a banister. He comments that as soon as he has put a rope around the neck of the film's villain he will put a ring on her finger, creating an association between the two forms of confinement. In films influenced by the female Gothic tradition, which include *Rebecca, Suspicion, Notorious, Shadow of a Doubt* (1943), *Dial M for Murder* (1953), and *Vertigo* (1958), marriage may result not only in the heroine's loss of control over her money and her life, but in some cases her identity. In both *Rebecca* and *Vertigo*, this process is linked specifically to the heroine's loss of control over her appearance: in *Rebecca* the nameless young wife is briefly ''made-over'' as the dead Rebecca, eliciting a violent reaction from her husband, and in *Vertigo* Judy dies after she loses control over her own masquerade and is made-over by Scottie. But the question of whether a woman *must* lose her sense of self when she marries is also posed in Hitchcock's work, for example in *Shadow of a Doubt*. Near the conclusion of the film, Emma Newton (Patricia Collinge) bids a tearful goodbye to her brother, saying, ''It's just that we were so close growing up. Then Charles went away and I got married. And, you know how it is, you sort of forget you're you. You're your husband's wife.'' As Elsie Michie has noted, the camera turns during this scene to Charlie (Theresa Wright), who is poised on the verge of accepting a marriage proposal herself.[34] The lingering close-up on Charlie's face indicates the ''shadow of a doubt'' cast over the institution of marriage not only by her mother's regretful comments, but also by her horror at the wife-murders of which she suspects her uncle.

Charlie can be seen to represent a new generation of women, separated from their mothers' traditional role by the experience of war and women's increasing autonomy outside the home. Yet she may also be, like Lisa Fremont and Francie Stevens, in love with a man who resists these changes in the balance of marital power. In Hitchcock's subsequent work, I would argue, such changes in gender roles are presented as part of modern life. But many of these films also imply that, for a man whose self-definition is dependent on traditional masculinity, to recognize femininity as a set of behaviors that can be modified or ''put on'' would precipitate an identity crisis (such as Scottie's breakdown in *Vertigo*). Hitchcock's postwar work has thus rightly been seen as preoccupied by a "postwar crisis in masculinity," but what has received less comment is that these films also feature heroines faced with a crisis around gender roles because of the apparent conflict between marriage and their own self-definition. Both Lisa and Francie cope with this situation through the tactical use of feminine behavior and appearances. As I've suggested in my readings of *Rear Window* and *To Catch a Thief*, however, this process simply underscores the performativity of gender roles, resulting in the films' somewhat tenuous romantic conclusions. The possible fragility of these marriages is also indicated in the 1956 version of *The Man Who Knew Too Much*, which, as Michie points out, explores the significant tensions within a married couple in which the heroine has given up a successful career in order to become a wife and mother.

Although the crisis in gender relations that Hitchcock's postwar work focuses on has often been analyzed in terms of patriarchal psychic structures, I would add that they are also quite historically specific and linked to broader social and political issues. In *North by Northwest*, for example, Hitchcock looks at some of the social forces that promote traditional masculinity. Roger Thornhill is a womanizing executive who is forced to take his "rightful" place in the state-sanctioned role of patriarch and warrior, substituting himself for the heroine, who has taken on that role out of necessity because men like Roger "don't believe in marriage." Thornhill's transformation into a "real" man not only saves Eve from her "masculine" work, it also helps save the U.S. from communism. In this film the institution of marriage not only ties women's identity to the role of wife and mother, it also ties male identity to the defense of the home and state. (In the train-station scene in which Thornhill finally separates from his mother and thus becomes fully masculine, a huge American flag hangs behind him and its colors become a dominant motif for the rest of the film's cold-war narrative.) The brilliance of Hitchcock's depiction of gender and performativity is not only in the way he shows the dependence of identity on gender norms, but the way he shows how gender roles are linked to the social division of labor and power.

The twin themes of mistaken identity and gender conflict that run throughout Hitchcock's work thus underscore the vulnerability of individuals to forces of social power (often in the form of government agents or police). There is an affinity among women like Lisa Fremont and Francie Stevens, who achieve their goals but only within the constraints of femininity, and men like Roger Thornhill, who gets his own identity back, but only by accepting the government's definition of his proper role. The concept of subjectivity is explicit in Hitchcock: characters are literally subject to definition by those in power, often in cruelly arbitrary ways (*The Wrong Man* is a kind of distillation of this theme.) The power relations behind identity are often recognized by women in Hitchcock's postwar films, but for the men the "unnatural" fragility of gender and identity usually comes as a great shock because they are so confident in their right to self-definition. Both Lisa and Francie show that they are inured to the state of "double consciousness" that comes from the tactical need to mask their equality with men. Their feminine masquerades thus describe not only the state of gender roles in the 1950s, but also illustrate the relationship between identity, gender, and social ideology.[35]

Notes

1. James Spada, *Grace: The Secret Lives of a Princess* (New York: Doubleday, 1987), 74.

2. Joan Rivière, "Womanliness as Masquerade," in *Formations of Fantasy*, ed. Victor Burgin, James Donald, and Cora Kaplan (London: Routledge, 1989), 38.

3. Erving Goffman, *The Presentation of Self in Everyday Life* (New York: Doubleday, 1959).

4. Edith Head, "Dialogue on Film," *American Film* 3, no. 7 (May 1978): 35.

5. Donald Spoto, *The Dark Side of Genius: The Life of Alfred Hitchcock* (Boston: Little, Brown and Company, 1983), 348.

6. "The New Gentle Look in American Fashion," *Vogue* (September 1, 1954), 174.

7. Elizabeth Wilson, *Adorned in Dreams: Fashion and Modernity* (London: Virago Press, 1985), 46.

8. Susan Smith, *Hitchcock: Suspense, Humor and Tone* (London: BFI, 2000), 77.

9. Smith, *Hitchcock: Suspense, Humor and Tone*, 77.

10. Richard Millington, "Hitchcock and American Character: The Comedy of Self-Construction in *North by Northwest*," in *Hitchcock's America*, ed. Jonathan Freedman and Richard Millington (New York: Oxford University Press, 1999), 140.

11. Paula Marantz Cohen, "Hitchcock's Revised American Vision: *The Wrong Man* and *Vertigo*," in *Hitchcock's America*, 155.

12. Cohen, "Hitchcock's Revised American Vision," 156; Amy Lawrence, "American Shame: *Rope*, James Stewart, and the Postwar Crisis in American Masculinity," in *Hitchcock's America*, 55-76.

13. Cohen, "Hitchcock's Revised American Vision," 169, 156

14. Michele Piso, "Mark's Marnie," in *A Hitchcock Reader*, ed. Marshall Deutelbaum and Leland Poague (Ames, Iowa: Iowa State University Press, 1986), 292.

15. Piso, "Mark's Marnie," 301.

16. Piso, "Mark's Marnie," 296, 297-98.

17. Robin Wood, *Hitchcock's Films*, third ed. (Cranbury, New Jersey: A.S. Barnes and Co., 1966), 72.

18. Elise Lemire, "Voyeurism and the Postwar Crisis of Masculinity in Rear Window," in *Alfred Hitchcock's* Rear Window, ed. John Belton (Cambridge: University of Cambridge Press, 2000), 77.

19. Tania Modleski, *The Women Who Knew Too Much: Hitchcock and Feminist Theory* (New York: Methuen, 1988), 84.

20. John Belton, "Spectacle and Narrative," in *Alfred Hitchcock's* Rear Window, 8.

21. François Truffaut, *Hitchcock*, revised ed. (New York: Touchstone, 1983), 223; Modleski, *The Women Who Knew Too Much*, 82.

22. Robert Stam and Roberta Pearson, "Hitchcock's *Rear Window*: Reflexivity and the Critique of Voyeurism," in *A Hitchcock Reader*, 204.

23. John Fawell, "Fashion Dreams: Hitchcock, Women, and Lisa Fremont," *Literature/Film Quarterly* 28, no. 4 (2000): 218.

24. Michele Piso, "Mark's Marnie," 292.

25. Elise Lemire, "Voyeurism and the Postwar Crisis of Masculinity in *Rear Window*," in *Alfred Hitchcock's Rear Window*, 85.

26. Piso, "Mark's Marnie," 300.

27. Peter Bogdanovich, *Who the Devil Made It* (New York: Knopf, 1997), 525.

28. "The Kelly's Cool Film Beauty," *Newsweek* (May 17, 1954), 96-101; "Hollywood's Hottest Property," *Life* (April 26, 1954), 117.

29. Truffaut, *Hitchcock*, 226.

30. Bogdanovich, *Who the Devil Made It*, 524.

31. Bogdanovich, *Who the Devil Made It*, 476.

32. Steven Cohan, *Masked Men: Masculinity and the Movies in the Fifties* (Bloomington: Indiana University Press, 1997), 17-18.

33. Spoto, *The Dark Side of Genius*, 352.

34. Elsie B. Michie, "Unveiling Maternal Desires: Hitchcock and American Domesticity," in *Hitchcock's America*, 48.

35. Thanks to Richard Allen and Sidney Gottlieb for their comments on an earlier draft of this essay, and to the students at the Australian Film, TV, and Radio School who shared their ideas on Hitchcock with me.

THE EMERGENCE OF AN AUTEUR: HITCHCOCK AND FRENCH FILM CRITICISM, 1950-1954

JAMES M. VEST

What enabled Eric Rohmer, François Truffaut, Claude Chabrol, and other writers for *Cahiers du Cinéma* in the 1950s to make the extraordinary claim that Alfred Hitchcock was more than a commercially-minded purveyor of melodramas? What led them to affirm that this entertainer was seriously engaged in creating a corpus of works with recurrent themes testifying to a coherent artistic vision and was therefore an *auteur de films*? What emboldened them to defend this claim tenaciously against all comers including the dean of French film critics, André Bazin, and even Hitchcock himself? Answers lie in the peculiar situation of postwar France where a number of interrelated factors, some of them material and social, others philosophical or even theological, coalesced to produce a matrix for the unthinkable: Hitchcock, auteur.[1]

Nearly two dozen Hitchcock films were screened commercially in France during the decade following the Liberation, as French audiences caught up on movies banned under the Occupation. The features Hitchcock made in America from 1940 to 1944, which had been *verboten* in Occupied France, were released there gradually after 1945. During the same period several vintage films from Hitchcock's British period were released commercially or shown at cinémathèques in Paris and Toulouse as part of retrospectives sponsored by French film societies. Consequently, between 1945 and 1954 French film buffs had access to more than twice as many Hitchcock films as did most of their American and British counterparts.

This cinematic avalanche in the late 1940s and early 1950s provoked an increase of discussion and debate among a number of highly articulate film enthusiasts. Their imagination and critical acumen were stimulated by the film clubs that sprang up all over France after the war and by a notable upswing in publications pertaining to cinema. Until 1949 many French-speaking cinephiles found inspiration in the venerable *Revue du Cinéma*, a glossy film magazine boasting quality photography and solid critical writing that thrived under the directorship of Jean George Auriol and, despite its intermittent publication history, had maintained its position as the preeminent forum for French film commentary since the late 1920s. Contributors to *La Revue du Cinéma* who wrote about Hitchcock's films, with varying degrees of admiration or disapproval, included Jacques Doniol-Valcroze, Auriol himself, and the earnest, energetic Maurice Schérer, who adopted the pseudonym Eric Rohmer.

The demise of *La Revue du Cinéma* in 1949 and the death of Auriol in 1950 left a void that was temporarily filled by several ephemeral publications. One was *Raccords*, a pocket-sized student magazine edited by Gilles Jacob, who would later write for *Cahiers du Cinéma* and *Positif*. *Raccords* featured provocative, mostly negative articles on Hitchcock by a number of young film enthusiasts, including Jacob himself and Oswald Ducrot, who, by faulting Hitchcock's camera work and editing, gave substance and sting to the phrase "le cas Hitchcock."[2] Another short-lived publication, *La Gazette du Cinéma*, was an unimposing newsletter of the Latin Quarter Film Club, edited by Rohmer. "Eight pages long, badly printed on mediocre paper, but full of ambition," the *Gazette* ran pieces by, among others, Alexandre Astruc and Jean-Paul Sartre as well as by newcomers Jacques Rivette and Jean-Luc Godard, writing as Hans Lucas.[3] In its ragged pages, the name Hitchcock would be linked, perhaps for the first time, with the ennobling epithet *auteur de films*.[4]

Numerous essays on Hitchcock found their way into the pages of a new monthly film magazine founded in April 1951 by Bazin, in conjunction with Doniol-Valcroze and Joseph-Marie Lo Duca. It sported a bright yellow cover and an auspicious title, *Cahiers du Cinéma*. Personally and professionally in Bazin's debt, cinephiles of various inclinations carried on intense debates in the pages of *Cahiers* about the importance, function, and future of cinema. They brought to their writings a passionate commitment to movies, a personalized style of commentary that emphasized judgments rooted in informed dialogue with filmmakers through carefully prepared interviews, and a dynamic aesthetic sensibility that soon focused on a controversial test case, "le cas Hitchcock."

French critics' reactions to Hitchcock's work varied widely. Chabrol, Rivette, Truffaut, and many of their contemporaries were intrigued and highly laudatory. Other commentators were less so. Among them were Bazin, the former *Revue du Cinéma* correspondent Herman G. Weinberg writing from New York, and "old-guard" critics such as Georges Charensol, Denis Marion, Jean Queval, and Georges Sadoul, writers who tended to view Hitchcock as at best a gifted technician with poor taste who had sold out to the American studio system.[5] Because of the revisionists' insistence that Hitchcock should be taken seriously, the traditionalists soon labeled them "Hitchcockiens fanatiques."[6] The stakes in the raging debate were raised as those "fanatical Hitchcockians" began to convince themselves that they detected in Hitchcock's works a pattern of consistent formal and conceptual traits that qualified this director as a bona fide cinematic auteur.

There was considerable division within *Cahiers* ranks as to whether Hitchcock deserved the title auteur, by which (on this point at least there was a degree of consensus) they meant a director who, by virtue of a uniquely personal artistic style and the will to impose it creatively, could be viewed as the unifying force behind a cinematic *œuvre*. For them an auteur was a creative artist, the conceiver and fabricator of a coherent imaginary world.[7] Their use of the term encouraged frequent comparisons of a film director's *œuvre* with the literary universes of Balzac or Shakespeare, Dostoevski or Faulkner. Truffaut and his allies asserted that Hitchcock fit this description nicely, and they took up arms to prove it.

Hitchcock received extensive coverage in *Cahiers* from the start. In its first issue Astruc boldly asserted that the much-maligned *Under Capricorn* conveyed a Miltonic sense of internal unity and an inestimable grace, "grâce au-delà de tous les calculs."[8] Noting in Hitchcock's work themes of grace extended and refused, and asserting more generally that the laws of cinema were also those of the soul, "les lois du cinéma sont celles de l'âme," Astruc linked film with theology and metaphysics.[9] Insisting that Hitchcock was a master filmmaker, Astruc posited literary and artistic comparisons with Corneille, Racine, Meredith, Henry James, Shakespeare, and even Bernini in an attempt to counter claims that Hitchcock had lost his touch. In the next month's issue Astruc was back with praise for *Stage Fright*, which he found prodigious in its use of ellipsis and visual portrayals of alibis. Claiming that relativity of truth constituted the essence of whodunits, Astruc defended the film's much-maligned "lying flashback."[10] The gauntlet had been thrown down, from a great height.

Weinberg, Bazin, and others took it up with verve. In his "Letter from New York" column, Weinberg suggested that the implausibilities and violence of *Strangers on a Train* constituted proof of Hitchcock's decline.[11] Perhaps sensing that a major storm was brewing and preferring to publish his negative assessments elsewhere than in *Cahiers*, Bazin returned in the pages of *L'Observateur* to a position he had previously announced in *L'Ecran Français*. With all the persuasiveness he could muster, Bazin insisted that Hitchcock's concern for technical effects far outweighed any interest the director might have either in humanistic themes or in the development of film as art.[12]

In the March 1952 issue of *Cahiers*, Godard strove for a middle ground, distancing himself from those who had nothing but "grande et continuelle admiration" for a director whom many others accused of lacking interest in plausibility.[13] Godard asserted that Hitchcock's films could contain no metaphysical subject matter for the simple reason that Hitchcock himself was the subject of all his films. Admitting that Hitchcock exercised a directorial virtuosity ranking him with Carl Dreyer and Abel Gance, Godard argued that

Hitchcock treated the modern condition, characterized by an attempt to escape from downfall without divine assistance, "la condition de l'homme moderne, qui est d'échapper à la déchéance sans le secours des Dieux," and hence he paradoxically qualified as a true realist, exemplifying realism of action.[14] A critical battle, he predicted prophetically, was likely to ensue. Although he was right about the conflict, Godard was mistaken on two points. He thought that the Hitchcockians could be counted on the fingers of one hand, and he believed that he could resist being drawn into their grip.

Those Hitchcockian "fanatics" were uncommonly vociferous and determined to be heard. Rohmer fired back with an article praising Hitchcock's handling of psychological displacement in *The Lady Vanishes* (released in France in 1952), which he considered extraordinary in its conception and execution.[15] Dismissing the usual complaints of detractors—superficiality, melodrama, technical considerations dominating expression—Rohmer pointed out the inconsistencies of critics who blamed Hitchcock for depicting the same sense of homelessness and absurdity that they praised in Kafka. Rohmer also noted that older Hitchcock films, including *The Lodger*, *Blackmail*, and *The 39 Steps*, had withstood the test of time, a rather remarkable accomplishment for a director categorized as a mere technician. In Rohmer's view Hitchcock qualified as a genius because of his expert depiction of suspicion and treatment of psychological displacement and of the absurd in ways that captured the malaise of modern life. Rohmer pronounced Hitchcock's films to be brilliant depictions of abnormal psychology, conceptually comparable to works by Dostoevski, that effectively moved from everyday commonality to the unexpected and from the improbable toward reality and therefore resisted becoming dated. Rohmer concluded that Hitchcock was "un des plus originaux et profonds auteurs," one of the most original and profound auteurs in the history of cinema.[16]

Soon Truffaut raised the stakes even higher. Responding to nay-sayers who continued to criticize Hitchcock's postwar work, he extolled *Under Capricorn* as the director's most beautiful film. In comments calculated to elicit a vigorous response on several fronts, Truffaut proposed Hitchcock as a worthy model for French filmmakers.[17] With such remarks definitive lines were insistently drawn for the ongoing critical battle.

Within a few months Rohmer returned to answer charges that *Cahiers* writers who favored Hitchcock's works represented a small, highly vocal "school" of criticism opposed to Bazin. He asserted that cinema was an art that should be seriously considered, with attention to structure as well as content. He proposed a sweeping defense of *Under Capricorn, Strangers on a Train*, and *I Confess*. This defense was rationally grounded in a "mode analogique," a comparative methodology that could be applied from one film to another.[18] Rohmer noted the existence of a discernible line, "une ligne très pure," connecting Hitchcock's films across the years and providing linkages that invited critics to view his work as a coherent, majestic fresco comparable to the literary creations of Balzac, Goethe, or Flaubert. Underscoring Hitchcock's attention to psychological themes with moral overtones, particularly through the leitmotifs of suspicion and self-discovery that pervaded his films, Rohmer formulated a two-part thesis central to the book that he would soon co-author with Chabrol: form was ineluctably linked to content for Hitchcock, and his films consistently depicted the spiritual at odds with the material as they portrayed courage and grace in opposition to unrestrained appetites and desires.

The "analogical" approach advocated by Rohmer was also invoked by Raymond Borde and Etienne Chumeton in their reviews of a Hitchcock retrospective sponsored by the Centre d'Etudes Cinématographiques in Toulouse. Borde and Chaumeton identified certain stylistic "constants," which were visible in Hitchcock's earlier films and which he was continually refining thereafter—an insistence on ellipsis, a penchant for symbolic objects, use of pleasurable sites (charity bazaars, amusement parks, theaters) as loci for mayhem, exceptionally stylized direction of actors—and concluded by calling him a true cinematic auteur, "un véritable auteur de films.''[19] Their observations advanced the concept of a Hitchcock canon, a coherent corpus of work characterized by humor, virtuosity, and infallible taste in pictorial detail.

Rivette took up the torch with a carefully-argued analysis of *I Confess* in terms of a delicate Hitchcockian equilibrium involving *exigence* and *inquiétude*, necessity and instability, that, Rivette asserted, proved cinema was the principal art form of the twentieth century.[20] Others, including Philippe Demonsablon, built on these ideas.[21] Thus the grounds for a sweeping thesis were articulated and gradually reinforced. In this evolving conception of Hitchcock, *auteur de films*, a specifically Cartesian approach was invoked in conjunction with an unfolding existential agenda.

◻   ◻   ◻   ◻   ◻

The ''Hitchcockiens fanatiques'' claimed to see patterns invisible to other eyes. Their peculiar perspective was attributable in part to the proliferation of cinemas, ciné-clubs, and cinémathèques leading to the concentrated availability of many Hitchcock films. It was also due to their particular disposition as committed cinephiles, whose enthusiasm for films knew no bounds. Truffaut and his companions adopted the habit of viewing films repeatedly, of absorbing them viscerally, of coming to know them intimately, as works of art. Their insights also resulted from the postwar caldron of ideas in which these critics used their classical training in Cartesian methodology and epistemology to confront emerging concepts of existential choice linked to evolving religious, social, political, and educational commitments.

Like their mentor Bazin, the Hitchcockians fused classical training in Cartesian methodology with a distinctly personal enthusiasm for cinema. They practiced Descartes' method of scientific analysis consisting of informed generalizations derived from iterated observations and grounded in systematic skepticism. Rohmer and his colleagues blended empirical methodology and inductive reasoning with the emerging concept of radical existential choice. Inspired by their tumultuous postwar social situation and by the time-honored Cartesian tradition that posited the existence of both a creative self and knowable constants, these cinephiles were prepared to observe in as much detail as possible the series of experiments projected onto movie screens around them, formulate hypotheses based on those observations, and validate their discoveries through animated discussion with anyone who expressed interest in their investigations. They were Cartesian not only in applying principles of hypothesis-building that moved from individual phenomena to general theses but also in asserting that it was possible through these activities to arrive at a coherent reflection of truth.[22] They were existentialist in their insistence on the ultimate importance of individualistic inventiveness and expression.

Truffaut's expertise in the areas of film history, filmography, and film facts was anchored in two Cartesian principles: detailed, multiple observations achieved by, in many cases, a dozen or more viewings of a film and careful data checks facilitated by an exhaustive archiving and cataloguing system, begun in his early teens, for classifying films by directors and movements. This systematic search for coherent structure and pattern, for consistent expressions of a thinking mind, led to Truffaut's emphasis on the director-writer as inventor of a cohesive cinematic œuvre, in Hitch-cock's case one revolving largely around paired situations and characters. This approach also inspired Rohmer's insistence on the primacy of form in Hitchcock's works and Chabrol's attention to Hitchcockian leitmotifs, including a recurrent struggle between good and evil involving a transfer of guilt. The Hitchcockians relied on Cartesian principles of investigation and analysis in their writings on and contacts with the filmmaker, as they found ways to combine information garnered in tape-recorded interviews with systematic argumentation, synthesizing their passionate love for cinema and a particular theological predisposition.

A major underlying factor in the developments that would define Cahiers du Cinéma in the mid-1950s was the

French church, which some *Cahiers* critics viewed as under attack by atheistic existentialism. With its emphasis on social reform and on cinema as a tool for education in the postwar era, Gallican Catholicism offered a theological and intellectual link between the Jesuit-trained Hitchcock and certain *Cahiers* commentators. Chief among them were Rohmer and Chabrol, who shared Hitchcock's penchant for what he labeled a Jesuit inclination toward "organization, control, and . . . analysis" as well as a particular emphasis on dualism and guilt.[23] Caught up in the tidal wave of debate surrounding the treatment of religious themes in Robert Bresson's *Diary of a Country Priest* (1951), Rohmer and Chabrol proceeded to address what they saw as comparable issues in Hitchcock's films, most notably the persistent conflict between good and evil, a haunting sense of culpability, and the need for confession.

Amid the intellectual and spiritual turmoil in the postwar years, with phenomenology, existentialism, absurdism, and secular humanism in the air, leaders of the Gallican church looked toward youth as a gauge of the future and to cinema as a means of instruction. Parochial schools were in a strategic position to reach children, teenagers, and young adults via organized showings and discussions of films. Film reviews and study guides as well as newsletters and fledgling periodicals aimed at teachers and youthful audiences were soon forthcoming from authorized sources. This context provided a natural matrix for discussion of Hitchcock as a Catholic filmmaker, particularly after the release of *I Confess*.

Anticlerical sentiment was also growing, and with it other new publications emerged, including *Cahiers du Cinéma*'s chief rival, *Positif*, founded in 1952. Whereas *Cahiers* was open to theoretical and metaphysical discussions, *Positif* tended to be more materialistic and much more socially engaged. *Positif* was staunchly anti-*Cahiers* and anti-Hitchcock. When it mentioned him at all, it was in a dismissive, deprecating way. From 1952 through 1955, *Cahiers* offered its readers over twenty articles and commentaries on Hitchcock, but in the same period *Positif* published only one, a diatribe by Louis Séguin entitled "Petit Bilan pour Alfred Hitchcock [A Little Reckoning for Alfred Hitchcock]," which summarily dismissed *Dial M for Murder* and *Rear Window* as "Jesuitical" drivel.[24]

Linked with this religious nexus was a lingering complex of national guilt resulting from France's ignominy during the war and from ongoing charges of collaboration with Nazis, issues that Hitchcock broached in his wartime films *Saboteur*, *Bon Voyage*, and *Aventure Malgache*, and again in 1954 in *To Catch a Thief*. In the mid-1950s France was still seeking closure to a traumatic epoch in its national consciousness. The Occupation, fresh in the minds of many, was commonly referred to euphemistically as "*that* period," a particularly shameful aspect of "a certain war." At the same time French cinema was grappling with the ascendancy of neorealism in Italy, a nation still viewed in some quarters as politically and socially suspect.

Reacting to postwar political and artistic trends and against the situationist claims of atheistic existentialism, Truffaut and his colleagues initiated a type of cinema criticism that was informed by traditional typologies, propelled by evolving social concerns, and imbued with the potentialities of self-expression. Then they molded it to their own polemical purposes as they proceeded to interpret "le cas Hitchcock" in terms of authorial creativity and a coherent "figure in the carpet" that had ethical as well as aesthetic overtones.[25] These children of the Second World War and intellectual descendants of Descartes, who contentiously blended an *esprit géométrique* and an *esprit de finesse* with hard-hitting personal commitment, perceived in Hitchcock's films a collection of motifs with geometrical, ethical, and metaphysical dimensions. Those motifs, they claimed, revolved around the related issues of binomial pairings and identity transfer, specifically the transfer of guilt.[26]

In the early 1950s Bazin and his protégés aggressively launched what Antoine de Baecque has labeled a "reasoned defense of critical taste."[27] Under Bazin's tutelage, the younger *Cahiers* writers came to see themselves not as movie reporters, but rather as critics and theorists in a grand tradition. Theirs was an august calling: to do for what Jean Cocteau called the youngest muse, something akin to what Voltaire, Diderot, Hugo, Baudelaire, and Breton, had done for her elder siblings.[28] Following Bazin's lead, Truffaut, Chabrol, and their *confrères* contemplated the origins, ontological status, and goals of an emerging art form that they considered ripe for explication. The dynamism of their theorizing was born of the immediate thrill of discovery grounded in their own viewing experiences as tempered by Cartesian skepticism. All of this came to a head when Truffaut launched the *politique des auteurs*.

□   □   □   □   □

In January 1954, twenty-one year old Truffaut published in the pages of *Cahiers* an impassioned appeal to reform French cinema, ''Une Certaine Tendance du cinéma français [A Certain Tendency of French Cinema].'' He blasted French films on the grounds that they were primarily formulaic adaptations designed to impress the festival juries at Cannes or Venice rather than original creations exploring uniquely filmic possibilities.[29] He accused prominent French directors and screenwriters of scorning cinema and its potential (the original title of this article, trimmed by Bazin, included the word ''mépris [scorn]''). In contrast Truffaut proposed a dynamic, personalized cinema of auteurs who were responsible for the stories and scripts on which their films were based as well as for many other aspects of cinematic *mise-en-scène*.[30]

Among the models for this *politique des auteurs* were Jean Cocteau, Abel Gance, Max Ophuls, Jean Renoir, Jacques Tati, Jean Vigo, and other directors who not only exercised a large degree of control over many phases of the production of their films but also imposed upon them a unique personal vision. It soon became clear that Truffaut was thinking of Hitchcock as well as of himself and other young would-be directors, whom he saw as capable of joining their ranks. While working on refining "Une Certaine Tendance" to the point where it would meet Bazin's standards for acceptance in *Cahiers*, a process that required months of revisions, Truffaut was also drafting his first screenplays and participating in his first filmed projects.[31] Thus, through Truffaut's searing polemic in *Cahiers*, the New Wave not only gave advance notice of its own birth but also articulated standards against which it ultimately would be judged.

With this 1954 article Truffaut rekindled the French "querelle des anciens et des modernes [Battle of the Ancients and the Moderns]," rejuvenating the classic dispute for the postwar generation and reorienting it toward a new subject: cinema. Truffaut's condemnatory invective shocked and offended, opened deep wounds, and unleashed a spate of responses. Reactions centered mostly on Truffaut's denigration of French productions while praising what many considered second-rate American fare, including Hitchcock's recent films.[32] *Cahiers* readers were passionately divided on this subject, as was the magazine's staff.

Some of the more heated debate centered on Hitchcock. The Hitchcockians' insistence on elevating this director to the status of auteur was particularly shocking because Hitchcock had been for so long dismissed as a venal spinner of thrillers— precisely the kind of movie maker Truffaut should scorn. Worse still, in postwar Britain, Hitchcock was viewed as something of a traitor (Had he not deserted his homeland in its darkest hour?), while in America he was considered a misplaced, misguided émigré (Why had he not applied for U.S. citizenship since moving to the States in 1939?). Yet he was heralded not only by Truffaut but also by Rohmer, Astruc, and Chabrol as an *auteur par excellence*. Their theories would be repeatedly tested in subsequent critical essays and in a series of now-famous interviews with Hitchcock in which issues of the ideal of the independent producer-writer-director were repeatedly raised. In the minds of Chabrol, Truffaut, and others associated with *Cahiers*, the name Hitchcock became synonymous with the heroic label "auteur," and they set about asserting that connection to the world, systematically.

□   □   □   □   □

Impelled by the personal predispositions described above and inspired by Cartesian methodology and a spate of recently-screened Hitchcock films, Truffaut and his fellow writers at *Cahiers* excitedly anticipated their first meeting with one who, they thought, could validate their hypotheses concerning thematic coherence in these works: the filmmaker himself. Hitchcock's extended visits to France during the production and post-production of *To Catch a Thief* (summer 1954 through late winter 1955) presented a golden opportunity for *Cahiers* critics to put their theories to the test.

As editor-in-chief of the magazine and its senior correspondent, Bazin would be the first to sally forth, traveling to the Riviera to observe filming of the flower market sequence in *To Catch a Thief* and to interview Hitchcock in Nice and again in Cannes. Those encounters yielded highly unsettling results that Bazin communicated to Truffaut and Chabrol and then to *Cahiers* readers. Over the next few months Chabrol and Truffaut would themselves take advantage of opportunities to interview Hitchcock in Paris on two occasions, with similarly distressing consequences. Their writings would convey the shock of their misapprehensions and of their perception of misrepresentation by Hitchcock. Their writings about their experiences with him would reveal profound disappointment in the interviewee, who blandly dismissed their serious questions while persistently engaging in "pirouettes" and "camouflage" tactics: Bazin would bristle at Hitchcock's feigned naiveté and superciliousness, Chabrol would speak of his interviewee's disingenuousness, and Truffaut would assert caustically "Hitchcock a menti [Hitchcock lied]."[33]

In an ironic twist worthy of a Hitchcock film, the theorists at *Cahiers* were keen to refine and test their hypotheses at precisely the same time the producer-director was preparing to initiate major enhancements to his public image. In these encounters with Hitchcock, evolving French critical sensibilities including the nascent *politique des auteurs* confronted the emerging Hitchcockian persona. That persona would soon crystallize through a number of new ventures, among them his highly successful Shamley Productions and a slew of publications and paraphernalia bearing his name, as well as his memorable weekly appearances on his popular television series. *Cahiers* writers attempting to validate their theories would play a unique role in creating a heady, unsettled atmosphere where there was ample room for maneuverings and posturings, thrusts and parries, misunderstandings and mistakes, and growth on all sides. Encounters in France between Hitchcock and the *Cahiers du Cinéma* staff resulted in a long-standing relationship that proved to be mutually beneficial, a unique connection that reoriented the future for all concerned.[34]

Notes

An earlier version of this essay was presented at the Hitchcock Centennial Conference sponsored by New York University, 16 October 1999. Portions of it will appear in the forthcoming collection of presentations from that conference, edited by Richard Allen and S. Ishii-Gonzalès. Material in this essay will be included in the author's forthcoming book, *Hitchcock and France*, to be published by Praeger; it appears here with permission of the copyright holder, James M. Vest, and of the publisher. Research for this project was facilitated by Faculty Development Grants from Rhodes College in 1998 and 1999. For their assistance the author is indebted to Nancy Vest, Cecelia Vest, Stéphanie Carrez, Mark Winokur, and David Mickle, as well as Paul Williford, Annette Cates, and William Short of Rhodes College Library, Joe Rees of Duke University Library, and the staffs of the British Film Institute, Bibliothèque de l'Arsenal, Bibliothèque du Film, and Bibliothèque de France.

1. Typical of Anglo-American criticism at mid-century was Lindsay Anderson's 1949 article on the filmmaker, in which he

stated that "Hitchcock has never been a serious director" and chastised him for his commercialism, superficiality, lack of realism, technical virtuosity for its own sake, and "stylistic elephantiasis" ("Alfred Hitchcock," *Sequence* no. 9 [autumn 1949]: 113-124; rpt. in *Focus on Hitchcock*, ed. Albert J. LaValley [Englewood Cliffs: Prentice-Hall, 1972]: 48-59; cited at 57-59). Contemporary critical opinions in France also tended to be condescending (e.g., Jean George Auriol, "Festival Hitchcock: *Shadow of a Doubt, Lifeboat.*" *Revue du Cinéma* N.S. 3, no. 15 [July 1948]: 64-70; and Jacques Doniol-Valcroze, "Festival Hitchcock: *Spellbound, Rebecca, Suspicion.*" *Revue du Cinéma*, N.S. 3, no. 15 [July 1948]: 72-77).

2. Oswald Ducrot, "Après *Le Procès Paradine*, le cas Hitchcock." *Raccords*, no. 1 (February 1950): 24-28.

3. Jean Douchet and Cédric Anger, *Nouvelle Vague*. Paris: Hazan/Cinémathèque française, 1998; translated into English by Robert Bonnono as *French New Wave* (Paris: D.A.P./Editions Hazan/Cinémathèque Française, 1998), cited at 88.

4. See Antoine de Baecque, "Avant-Propos," *La Revue du cinéma: anthologie* (Paris: Gallimard, 1992), v.

5. For a roster of principal combatants, see Chabrol "Les Choses sérieuses," *Cahiers du Cinéma*, no. 46 (April 1955): 41n. In the text of my essay, the shortened form *Cahiers* will be used to refer to *Cahiers du Cinéma*. All English translations from the French are my own.

6. The phrase is Bazin's in "Hitchcock contre Hitchcock," *Cahiers du Cinéma*, no. 39 (October 1954): 30; cf. "ses plus farouches partisans [his fiercest partisans]" and "des Hitchcockiens maximalistes [Hitchcockians to the max]" (25).

7. Based on Astruc's notion of *caméra-stylo* [the camera as writing instrument], the concept of the auteur involved both distinctive style and masterly manipulation of themes (see Douchet, *New Wave*, 98); citing Hitchcock as an example, Douchet makes the point that although an auteur might be involved in personal oversight of script writing and other aspects of production, this was not always the case (105).

8. Alexandre Astruc "Au-dessous du volcan," *Cahiers du Cinéma*, no. 1 (April 1951): 29-33, cited at 30.

9. Astruc, "Au-dessous du volcan," 29.

10. Alexandre Astruc, "Alibis et ellipses," *Cahiers du Cinéma*, no. 2 (May 1951): 50-51.

11. Herman G. Weinberg, *Cahiers du Cinéma*, no. 6 (October-November 1951): 33.

12. André Bazin, "Faut-il croire en Hitchcock?" *L'Observateur*, no. 88 (January 1952): 23-24; in his earlier critique, "Panoramique sur Hitchcock," in *L'Ecran Français*, no. 238 (23 January 1950): 8-9, Bazin concluded that Hitchcock had made no significant contributions to cinematic *mise-en-scène* in over a decade.

13. Jean-Luc Godard [Hans Lucas], "Suprématie du sujet," *Cahiers du Cinéma*, no. 10 (March 1952): 59-61, cited at 59.

14. Godard "Suprématie," 59-60.

15. Eric Rohmer, "Le Soupçon," *Cahiers du Cinéma*, no. 12 (May 1952): 63-65.

16. Rohmer, "Le Soupçon," 64-65.

17. François Truffaut, "Les Extrêmes me touchent," *Cahiers du Cinéma*, no. 21 (March 1953): 61-62.

18. Eric Rohmer, "De Trois Films et d'une certaine école," *Cahiers du Cinéma*, no. 26 (August-September 1953): 22.

19. Raymond Borde and Etienne Chaumeton, "Flash-back sur Hitchcock" *Cahiers du Cinéma*, no. 17 (November 1952): 58.

20. Jacques Rivette, "L'Art de la fugue," *Cahiers du Cinéma*, no. 26 (August-September 1953): 49-52.

21. Philippe Demonsablon, "Visage de l'amoureuse," *Cahiers du Cinéma*, no. 30 (December 1953): 16-21, and Rivette, "L'Age des metteurs en scène," *Cahiers du Cinéma*, no. 31 (January 1954): 48.

22. These procedures correspond to the first three steps of the four outlined by Descartes in his *Discours de la méthode* (1637), a text familiar to every schoolchild in France. The final step, that of continuing investigative checks drawing on research involving disparate sources, characterized the critical method of the *Cahiers* writers in question in the 1950s.

23. Hitchcock's comments on the long-term influence of his Jesuit education were included in Peter Bogdanovich, *The Cinema of Alfred Hitchcock* (New York: Museum of Modern Art/Doubleday, 1963), 9.

24. Louis Séguin, "Petit Bilan pour Alfred Hitchcock: *Le Crime était presque parfait, Fenêtre sur cour*," *Positif*, no. 14-15 (November 1955): 62-64.

25. Claude Chabrol, "Histoire d'une interview," *Cahiers du Cinéma*, no. 39 (October 1954): 42-44.

26. See, for example, François Truffaut, "Un Trousseau de fausses clés," *Cahiers du Cinéma*, no. 39 (October 1954): 45-53; and Claude Chabrol, "Hitchcock devant le mal," *Cahiers du Cinéma*, no. 39 (October 1954): 18-24.

27. Antoine de Baecque, *Les Cahiers du Cinéma: Histoire d'une revue*. 2 vols. (Paris: Cahiers du Cinéma, 1991), 1:14.

28. One of Jean Cocteau's drawings bears the phrase "Vive cette jeune muse, cinéma" alongside a sketch of an ecstatic young woman among stars; cf. Rohmer who called cinema "le dernier-né des arts [the youngest of the arts]" (*Cahiers du Cinéma*, no. 51, October 1955: 6). The other authors listed here were prominent in furthering aesthetic theory in France from the eighteenth century through the age of surrealism.

29. François Truffaut, "Une Certaine Tendance du cinéma français," *Cahiers du Cinéma*, no. 31 (January 1954): 15-24.

30. Truffaut, "Une Certaine Tendance," 23-29.

31. Bazin repeatedly delayed publishing this incendiary essay that Truffaut had first drafted in 1951; the decision to print it in *Cahiers* was a courageous one because of its strident tone and predictably unsettling impact on traditionalists, including critics and filmmakers who were personal friends of Bazin. On the various drafts of this article, which over the course of three years went from scattered notes to a thirty-one-page treatise and finally to the terse attack published in *Cahiers*, see Antoine de Baecque and Serge Toubiana, *Truffaut*, trans. by Catherine Temerson (New York: Knopf, 1999), 63-72.

32. For details of the controversy that ensued, see Antoine de Baecque, "Contre la Qualité française: Autour d'un article de François Truffaut," *Cinémathèque* 4 (fall 1993): 53-59, and de Baecque and Toubiana, 72-77.

33. These comments appeared in three articles published in *Cahiers*, no. 39 (October 1954), an issue devoted to Hitchcock: Bazin, "Hitchcock contre Hitchcock," 26-30; Chabrol, "Histoire d'une Interview," 40; Truffaut, "Un Trousseau de fausses clés," 50.

34. For an analysis of how this dynamic of creating his persona by a combination of his own efforts and those of his critics worked, from Hitchcock's perspective, see Robert E. Kapsis, "Hitchcock: Auteur or Hack? How the Filmmaker Reshaped his Reputation Among the Critics," *Cineaste*, 14, no. 3 (January 1986): 30-35.

Gus Van Sant vs. Alfred Hitchcock: A *Psycho* Dossier

Introduction by Richard Allen

In 1998, American film director Gus Vant Sant remade Hitchcock's *Psycho* (1960) for Universal Studios in a manner that has no precedent in the history of film. While of course Van Sant employed a new group of actors to play the original roles, he mimicked, though not entirely, the original script of *Psycho*, Hitchcock's camera set-ups, and his editing patterns. Vant Sant, it seems, decided to imagine that Hitchcock's film was a like a play for which he would provide a new interpretation, a new performance. A play, though, is realized only through the discreet instances of its performance. There exists no original performance against which a given interpretation can be measured: there are at best ''canonical'' performances. The ''performance'' of a film, however, is embodied in a mass-produced artifact that constitutes the artwork, in this case Hitchcock's *Psycho*. Van Sant's experiment of rendering anew Hitchcock's *Psycho* on film is thus one that enjoins us to compare it with the original, indeed, whose *raison d'etre* is the relationship that it bears to the original.

Apart from its cinematic virtues or liabilities, Van Sant's *Psycho* raises questions that are vital to Hitchcock scholarship, of which it may itself be a peculiar instance. What does the existence of Van Sant's *Psycho* tells us about the status of Hitchcock and *Psycho* in the history of film, and the reception of his work within contemporary culture? What are the features of Hitchcock's work in general, as well as of *Psycho* in particular, that lend themselves to this kind of appropriation? What does the existence of a remake reveal about the relationship between the practices of commercial cinema and those of contemporary art? What does a comparison between Hitchcock's and Van Sant's films illuminate about the nature of Hitchcock's achievement in

Psycho, Van Sant's own preoccupations as an auteur, and the value of the remake? These are among the subjects addressed from a wide range of critical perspectives and within a purposely brief compass by the contributors to this dossier, conceived of and assembled by Steven Jay Schneider and Constantine Verevis.

THE ARTIST PAYS HOMAGE

PAULA MARANTZ COHEN

The question of how to pay homage to a great work or to a great artist has been a vexed one ever since literary criticism became a legitimate academic activity at the beginning of the twentieth century. This was when it became necessary to distinguish an enduring, "objective" perspective on a text from a more ephemeral, subjective one (the kind associated with the commercial reviewer). Personal admiration for a work or an artist had to go undercover, as it were. The entire history of literary criticism and its offshoot, film criticism, can be understood as an elaborate method of finding universalist criteria to support such admiration. Thus New Criticism supported admiration for the metaphysical poets; Freudian criticism for the Romantics; Structuralism for the Modernists; and New Historicism for Shakespeare and the Victorians. Auteur theory, the one distinct mode of film theory not directly borrowed from literary theory, can be said to have arisen so that French intellectuals could express their love for the American movies that deluged France following the Occupation.

The concept of homage has only gone more undercover with the rise of Deconstructionist theory and the presumed death of the author. We see the tortuous turns required in Peter Wollen's famous declaration that "Fuller or Hawks or Hitchcock, the directors, are quite separate from 'Fuller' or 'Hawks' or 'Hitchcock,' the structures named after them, and should not be methodologically confused."[1] Great men are not to be admired, Wollen implies, but we can still pay homage to great structures. Of course, Deconstruction might also be interpreted as an ingenious way for critics to pay homage to themselves.

And yet, though the death of the author has seemed imminent for years, it has apparently not yet been fully realized. Despite theoretical efforts to the contrary, there persists a desire, even on the part of academic critics, to pay tribute to works and the producers of works (and not just to structures) that give enduring pleasure and yield complex meaning.

Evidence for this regarding that preeminent auteur, Alfred Hitchcock, was the gala "Celebration" in honor of the centennial of his birth organized by the NYU Cinema Studies Department in 1999. That Celebration (and the title in itself reflects an uncharacteristic academic willingness to pay homage) was a strange or perhaps prescient mix of detached theorizing and straight-out gushing. Cheek by jowl with the academic papers (some of them in French) were featured appearances by old actresses waxing nostalgic, screenwriters inclined to gossip, and Hitchcock's daughter, a quasi-royal personage, whose presence served, rather in the opposite of Derridean erasure, to verify the fact that her father had indeed existed.

Absent from the festivities, with the exception of a potshot here and there, was reference to the recent remake of *Psycho* by Gus Van Sant. The film was an enigma to popular and academic critics alike, who could not for the life of them figure out why so much money would be spent to make a shot-by-shot reenactment of the original with a few minor deviations. And yet, I would argue, the film deserved pride of place at the Celebration. It is the consummate homage to the Master.

Generally, the rationale for a remake falls into one of two categories. One is when a filmmaker chooses to use a work as the basis for what is essentially a new artistic creation. Here the idea of the remake loosens to become something closer to an adaptation. John Huston's *Maltese Falcon* (1941), a masterful reconstruction of the lackluster 1931 version of Dashiell Hammett's novel, is an example. The 1940 *His Girl Friday*, Howard Hawks's highly cinematic rethinking of the more mechanical 1931 stage adaptation, *The Front Page*, is another example, as is Hitchcock's 1956 remake of his own 1934 version of *The Man Who Knew Too Much*. In the case of these works, we can apply Harold Bloom's theory of influence, and say that the "strong poet" who "misreads" the work of a literary precursor becomes the strong poet-filmmaker who misreads a cinematic precursor.[2] (In Hitchcock's case, in typically outsized fashion, he misread himself—or, to be more precise, the American Hitchcock misread the British Hitchcock.) The weak filmmaker, by contrast, cannot fully incorporate the source, and the original film is likely to show through, to exist in undigested clumps that jar with the new film—as is often the case in Brian De Palma's use of Hitchcock, for example.

However, there is another, more common kind of remake that has nothing to do with artistic appropriation. It happens for purely commercial reasons. The assumption is that the original can no longer appeal to a contemporary audience, which will have no patience for stylistic elements (e.g., dress, décor, idioms of speech) that have changed with time. It is thought that by merely updating these elements and taking advantage of technological or casting gimmicks, then box-office success can be assured. Remakes of this sort also obliterate the originals upon which they are based, not because they are the work of strong poet-filmmakers but because the results are too negligible to evoke their sources. They seem to operate in another realm and activate an entirely different set of viewing responses. This is most marked in television remakes of feature films, of which Hitchcock has been a noted victim. A recent example, the Christopher Reeve *Rear Window*, makes my point succinctly.

Yet the Van Sant *Psycho* hardly falls into either of the above categories. It is not intended (at least not obviously) to eclipse the original and imprint a new signature upon it. Neither is it (at least not primarily) a commercial venture, attempting to take advantage of the popularity and success of the original film.

Instead, I would argue that Van Sant is engaged in something akin to the kind of homage paid to literature and film by the professional critic, though operating in a visual as opposed to a literary medium. For what the film succeeds in doing above all is bringing us back to the original and displaying both its structure and what Andrew Sarris might call its "elan of the soul."[3] One has only to look at the review of the film by Roger Ebert in the *Chicago Sun-Times* to measure its success in this regard. Writes Ebert: "Curious, how similar the new version is, and how different. . . . Genius apparently resides between or beneath the shots, or in chemistry that cannot be timed or counted."[4] Though he has put the difference down to an ineffable quality of genius, Ebert then goes on to do a point-by-point analysis of the disparity between original and remake—from the shower scene (a fuzzier shot of the stuffed birds in the remake destroys "the feeling that they're poised to swoop"), to the peephole scene (the sound effects that accompany Van Sant's explicit addition of masturbation "inspire a laugh at the precise moment when one is not wanted"), to the casting (Vaughn "isn't odd enough"; Anne Heche "lacks the carnal quality and the calculating detachment that Janet Leigh brought to the original film"). And so on.

In "Remaking *Psycho*," James Naremore engages in a more extended and academic version of what Ebert does here. Naremore, too, frames his analysis of the Van Sant film with a more general observation, in this case a comparison of his experience of the original film at its release at the local theater in New Orleans ("galvanically terrifying") with his response to the remake ("Van Sant's film strikes me as academic and not at all scary").[5] He then goes on to organize his discussion of Van Sant's film into a comparison with the original based on the components of script, casting and acting, sound, photography, editing and camera movement, and *mise-en-scène* and production design—always, of course, to the advantage of Hitchcock. Naremore concludes that "A better solution would have been to simply remaster the original 35mm print and exhibit it around the world"—to which he immediately adds: "A new print of *Psycho* will in fact be shown this year in New York, as part of the Hitchcock centennial celebration at NYU."[6] But perhaps the Van Sant film inspired that new print and its screening at the NYU Celebration just as it precipitated Ebert and Naremore's reviews. Indeed, isn't the attention to Hitchcock generated by the Van Sant remake an homage to the original film similar to the homage represented by showing the original at the NYU Celebration? For as Naremore notes, no contemporary screening of the film can possibly reproduce the "galvanically terrifying" experience that he and others felt on first viewing it, which leads him to the conclusion: "For all its continuing interest, *Psycho* is no longer a cutting-edge horror film."[7] Any reshowing of the original is therefore, by necessity, a form of homage rather than a recreation of the original experience. As for Van Sant's film, it is a mechanism for catalyzing homage, as ingeniously designed to draw admiring attention to the original as anything Hitchcock might have come up with himself.

It may seem odd, of course, that a Hollywood director or, for that matter, a creative artist, would be willing to abase himself in the service of a predecessor—for homage has traditionally involved self-abasement. Self-abasement goes against the Oedipal thrust of the creative urge, as Bloom would argue, and, even more, it goes against the hubris that we all know to be endemic to Hollywood. And yet homage may have undergone a mutation in our post-postmodern age, allowing it to accommodate both the creative and commercial aspect that it had traditionally placed itself on the one hand, below and, on the other, above.

If we accept Arthur Danto's argument in *After the End of Art: Contemporary Art and the Pale of History*, then self-consciousness in and of itself—the awareness of the cultural greatness (if not the absolute greatness) of Hitchcock's *Psycho*, in the case under discussion here—becomes its own artistic contribution.[8] This is another turn on the self-aggrandizement of the critic that has been the thrust of postmodern criticism; it simply adds the observer as well as the critic into the equation. Danto dates this last stage in the development of art to Warhol's *Brillo Box*, where the artistic work merely duplicates, in point by point detail, a mundane object in the world. In recent lectures, Danto has taken this point further and made it even more relevant to Van Sant's film. He addresses Paul Theck's imitations of Warhol's *Brillo*

Box, which he connects to an entire school of photographic imitation, most notably Sherry Levine's photographs of Margaret Bourke-White's acclaimed Depression-era photographs. The imitations are different from the originals they imitate because they exist in a new context that includes the awareness of the viewer of their relationship to great or culturally important art. Thus imitation can be reclaimed as a form of philosophical art (call it art merged with criticism) while maintaining its function as homage.

It is perhaps the hallmark of the artist at the end of art to want to have it all: to be commercially successful and artistically respectable, to honor past greatness and to assert one's own priority in the present, to be both creator and critic. Van Sant, commercial blockbuster director and serious *artiste*, has produced, with his remake of *Psycho*, a work of homage that is also the consummate hybrid of art and criticism at the present time.

Notes

1. Peter Wollen, "The Auteur Theory," in Leo Braudy and Marshall Cohen, eds., *Film Theory and Criticism: Introductory Readings*, 5th ed. (New York: Oxford University Press, 1999), 532.

2. Harold Bloom, *The Anxiety of Influence: A Theory of Poetry* (New York: Oxford University Press, 1973).

3. Andrew Sarris, "Notes on the Auteur Theory in 1962," in Braudy and Cohen, eds., *Film Theory and Criticism*, 517.

4. Roger Ebert, "*Psycho*," http://www.suntimes.com/ebert/ebert_reviews/1998/12/120601.html (July 2, 2001).

5. James Naremore, "Remaking *Psycho*," *Hitchcock Annual* (1999-2000), 4, 5.

6. Naremore, "Remaking *Psycho*," 12.

7. Naremore, "Remaking *Psycho*," 12

8. Arthur C. Danto, *After the End of Art: Contemporary Art and the Pale of History* (Princeton: Princeton University Press, 1997).

SHOT-BY-SHOT FOLLIES

ADRIAN MARTIN

Jeanne Moreau: I ask why our society needs all these copies of things. Not just paintings. Copies of everything. Even things like clothes, suitcases, bags, watches . . .

Marcello Mastroianni: I believe that anyone copying the works of a great artist has a chance of repeating the artist's actions and possibly recapturing, even by chance, his precise gesture.

Moreau: A copy of the gesture.

Mastroianni: And why not? Recapturing the gesture of a genius would give me more satisfaction than any brushstrokes of my own.

—dialogue from *Beyond the Clouds*
(Michelangelo Antonioni/Wim Wenders)

There sometimes arises, in the cinema studies world, a vast disparity between the quality of a certain film and the quantity of earnest discourse that it prompts. Nowhere has this disparity been so striking as in the case of Gus Van Sant's 1998 remake of Alfred Hitchcock's *Psycho*.

Van Sant's film is a dismal experience. No amount of clever justification or hair-splitting—about it being a conceptualist artwork, a cheeky subversion of the studio system, a post-classical recasting of a classic, an ultimate gesture of homage, a postmodern appropriation, a staging of cultural differences, an exercise in hyperreal aesthetics, or a work that forces us to rethink the philosophical status of remakes—can tempt me to ever watch it again. Indeed, I can hardly believe that, almost three years after its release, we are still talking about it here.

The only noteworthy aspect of Van Sant's folly is what its "experiment" proves: that you can mechanically copy all the surface moves of a screen classic and still drain it of any meaning, tension, artistry, and fun. Van Sant claimed, at the moment of the film's release, that he hoped to introduce Hitchcock's masterpiece to a young generation of filmgoers reared on TV and video; unfortunately, this audience is likely to be now wondering why *Psycho* is any more worthy of their attention than *Scream 2* (1997) or *Halloween H20* (1998).

Everything about the project is badly misjudged. Pre-release hype stressed that Van Sant took the same amount of time to shoot as Hitchcock did; that he brought in the original writer, Joseph Stefano, to lightly revise the script; that Bernard Herrmann's magnificent musical score was re-recorded under the supervision of Danny Elfman. But so what? The so-called modernizations instituted by Van Sant—explicit sexual references; a couple of contemporary nods to pop culture and modern technology; several interpolations of hallucinatory imagery; added audio effects—amount to no more than vague doodling in the margins of the original's image and sound tracks, a less than arresting "remix."

Despite the attempt to subtly drag Hitchcock's material into the present day, everything still has a weird early 1960s aura. This caused the audience I watched it with (in Australia in early 1999) to laugh derisively at both Van Sant's modern touches (like a character wearing a Walkman) and the manifest "corniness" of Hitchcock's original, with its prurient references to bathrooms and bodily functions, and its ham-fisted speeches about the evil in men's hearts and minds. Van Sant has managed neither homage nor critique; he neither respects Hitchcock's artistic point-of-view (or the cultural, generic and compositional elements with which he necessarily worked in his time), nor advances his own.

This new *Psycho* feels, more than anything, like a desultory "walk through," a listless restaging that demonically turns the original, retroactively, into a stuffed museum exhibit. The cast members are constrained to stand in the same positions as their predecessors and utter (more or less) the same lines; as a result, their performances are hopelessly wooden and superficial. The same applies to the contribution of cinematographer Chris Doyle, whose natural penchant for lyrical movement and vibrant color (evident in his work for Wong Kar-Wai) is cruelly curtailed.

Certain highly intellectual critics like (or are at least intrigued by) this film for one reason alone that I can fathom: it is exactly the kind of movie that critics themselves would make if suddenly allowed to do so. Van Sant put himself precisely in the position of a "textual analyst," 1970s-style, when he came up with the idea of a so-called "shot-by-shot" remake of *Psycho*.

Let me explain this contention. Only those who do not make films perceive them as existing shot by shot, i.e., in discrete shot units. This is the myopia that academic textual analysis teaches: count the cuts and "segment" the scene appropriately. In a strange synchronicity with Van Sant's *Psycho*, another blast from the past hit Anglo-American cinema studies not so far from the time of the film's release: the shortened translation, twenty years late, of Raymond Bellour's *The Analysis of Film*, a work which, as it happens, is centrally concerned with Hitchcock, and also with the protocols of shot-by-shot breakdown.

This collection of essays is a masterpiece of 1970s-style textual analysis. Bellour divides, computes, and cross-references shot-units with a minute systematicity that (as he frankly avows) borders on obsessiveness, even madness. What matters for him is the internal, fine-grain evolution that makes one unit in a tabulated shot list different from those that surround it: a difference in speed, for instance; a difference in movement or stasis, in sound or silence; a difference based on whether the shot is an opening, a prolongation, or a closing of the scene; a difference based on the shot's position within a graph of successive alternations that produce pattern and meaning.

All of this—at least in Bellour's hands, if not in those of his dreariest disciples—is fascinating, even thrilling. Bellour, a gifted writer, never lost sight of the fact that he was ultimately composing a kind of analytical *roman*, a fiction of ideas. In a turn of phrase not uncommon in his work, he prefaces his 1969 treatment of a sequence from *The Birds*

(1963): "Analysis forces me and structure invites me to divide the sequence into registerable segments."[1] Yet we can nonetheless find, hidden inside this first major essay in textual analysis by Bellour on Hitchcock, a fleeting qualification that the author sweeps past, and that none of his subsequent followers seem to have ever noted. "A sequence, then—once the word is merely conventional and reveals itself to be as inadequate to designate a fixed unit of narration as the shot is for a fixed unit of photography"; a note then refers us to Jean Mitry on "the ambiguities of the definition of the shot."[2]

What, then, is so (intellectually) conventional, inadequate, and ambiguous about shot-by-shot analysis? The problem is that, quite simply, films are not made shot by shot. Most films, certainly most narrative films, are built upon the unit of the scene (a nominal unity or convergence of time, action, and place, however disunified these elements may later become in post-production), and the filming of that scene is arrived at via the process of "coverage," deciding from which camera set-ups the action is to be recorded. It is in the "blocking out" of the scene, before the cameras roll—the staging of the actor's movements, gestures, and lines—that set-ups come to be decided. Some cuts between set-ups might be foreseen well in advance, but mostly those decisions are left to the editing phase, when many possible permutations of all set-ups filmed are entertained. Trying to reconstitute the set-ups in any given scene—and sorting out the difference between master shots, inserts, and so on, which is basic film craft—is rarely part of the protocol of textual analysis, even though it is in this particular kind of shot economy that the ingenuity of certain directors (including low-budget wizards such as Peter Greenaway, Olivier Assayas, and early Brian De Palma) is best revealed.[3]

This is the cinema of *mise-en-scène* as practiced by everyone from F.W. Murnau and Kenji Mizoguchi to Arthur Penn and André Téchiné. Its analysis (in my view) should aim to reconstitute and interpret a veritable polyphony of pertinent rhythms, flows, intensities, movements, punctuations, modulations, and patterns in a scene—built from gesture, action, music, image-sound relations, camera mobility, and so on—in which cuts figure as only one variable among many, and not necessarily the most determining. Beginning from the nominal unity of the scene (which is itself only ever a "conventional" starting point), we then build our apprehension of this form and content polyphony to recreate ever larger segments or ensembles, until we arrive at the shape and logic of the whole film.

Of course, we can find many exceptions to this rather classical aesthetic within experimental fields—for example, clear shot-by-shot works such as Alain Cavalier's *Libera Me* (1993), a film solely comprised of stand-alone inserts and portrait shots. In discussing such formal inventions more recently, Bellour himself usefully refers to a plurality of practices (*mise-en-pages, mise-en-phrases, mise-en-place, mise-en-plans, mise-en-images,* and *mise-en-plis*) beyond the conventional unities and possibilities of *mise-en-scène*.[4] At a certain point, such speculative games displace us beyond cinema altogether, and we find ourselves in the rarefied realms of digital multimedia or installation art—precisely the kinds of realms in which Van Sant's *Psycho* has found its most natural echo, and its staunchest defenders. As anyone who has strolled through a gallery of modern art in the past decade knows, this world is full of mutant, deformed, gleefully appropriated "Hitchcocks."

But where does the real artist and craftsman Hitchcock stand in all this discussion of "the shot"? Although the longstanding myth of Hitchcock as the manic storyboard artist might seem to return us, by the back door, to a shot-by-shot model, Bill Krohn's invaluable research in *Hitchcock at Work* has established once and for all that the director exploited to the hilt the looseness and variability that came with *mise-en-scène* shooting.[5] Likewise, according to a recent documentary, Stanley Kubrick—whose taste for visual and dramatic geometry might suggest another rigidly "predetermining," shot-by-shot stylist—never fixed his shots until after much open-ended work with the actors.[6]

By adopting the madness of the "shot-by-shot remake," Van Sant has denied himself the flexibility—even the very possibility—of arriving at his own *mise-en-scène*. There are no natural or pleasing movements, rhythms, or patterns of any sort in his version of *Psycho*; the actors are constrained to always pose in or arrive at preset positions in the frame that are slavishly copied from a monitor or a storyboard reproducing the original. The evident strain of this rigid, conceptual exercise in fragmented staging explains the awesome sluggishness and unpersuasiveness of the final result.

In Jorge Luis Borges' famous story "Pierre Menard, Author of the Quixote," long ago adopted as an emblem of zany postmodern creativity, a writer manages to spontaneously produce fragments of text identical to passages in Cervantes.[7] Critics hail the result as in fact superior to the original, since it speaks so much more vibrantly to its contemporary, historical moment. Was Van Sant's dream to stumble upon a similar kind of fool's gold? Sadly for him—and us—the difference between his *Psycho* and Hitchcock's can be exactly pinpointed in that famous shower scene and its immediate aftermath. Where, in the original, the sudden execution of Marion disorientated audiences and cagily rerouted the narrative, here the passage from a minutely recreated "classic" scene of violence to another piece of plot more closely resembles Van Sant lazily flicking channels on his TV remote control—only to find an even less interesting program.

Notes

1. Raymond Bellour, *The Analysis of Film* (Bloomington: Indiana University Press, 2000), 30.
2. Bellour, *The Analysis of Film*, 29, 284.
3. One of the few canonical pieces of film criticism to address the complex relationship between camera set-ups and cutting is Brian Henderson's 1971 essay "The Long Take," reprinted in *A Critique of Film Theory* (New York: Dutton, 1980), 48-61, with its

(sadly unadopted) terminology of the "intrasequence cut" and "*mise-en-scène* cutting" in Ophuls, Mizoguchi, and Welles.

4. Raymond Bellour, "Figures aux allures de plans," in Jacques Aumont, ed., *La mise en scène* (Bruxelles: De Boeck, 2000), 109-26.

5. Bill Krohn, *Hitchcock at Work* (London: Phaidon, 2000).

6. See *Stanley Kubrick: A Life in Pictures*, directed by Jan Harlan, 2001.

7. Jorge Luis Borges, *Labyrinths*, trans. James E. Irby and Donald A. Yates (London: Penguin, 1970), 62-71.

VAN SANT THE PROVOCA(U)TEUR

STEVEN JAY SCHNEIDER

At least for half of the audience or so, are they watching two movies at the same time in their mind? Are they really watching both movies, sort of making quick comparisons constantly?

—Philip Baker Hall[1]

Interviewer: Do you ever stand back and watch your films and go, "I can see how I do it?" *Van Sant*: I can see stuff. I usually try to change it, though. A lot of times when you try and change it, it doesn't really change. You know, you think, I have this thing going and then you step out and try and do something like *Good Will Hunting*, which is not like my other movies. And then, at the same time, it sort of looks like your movies even though you were trying really hard. *Interviewer*: You were trying to make it different? *Van Sant*: I was trying to make it not like something that I would do. But because you're making the decisions it ends up being like one of your movies.[2]

Reaction from journalists and scholars alike to Gus Van Sant's more or less shot-for-shot remake of *Psycho* (1998) has been remarkably consistent in its disapproval. Virtually all the changes made to Hitchcock's 1960 version have been criticized as for the worse, and despite some crumbs thrown Van Sant's way—William Rothman deems him a director "not devoid of talent,"[3] and James Naremore calls him a "respectable filmmaker with several fine films to his credit"[4]—the assumption from the start seems to have been that he had no chance whatsoever of beating the Master of Suspense at his own game. A remark by Esther Anatolitis goes some way towards explaining why the dominant mode of analysis of the remake of *Psycho* has been one of negative contrast: "What Van Sant achieves is to force the viewer into looking for differences within a field of repetition, where other remakes have us desperately looking for similarities and elbowing our friends in the darkened cinema when we recognize the ever-so-oblique references, so very proud of our sharpness."[5]

Implicit or explicit in the many strikingly (yet boringly) similar discussions of Van Sant's *Psycho* is the belief that Hitchcock was an auteur director, someone with at least a sufficient degree of authorial control over all relevant aspects of his films. Evidence of this control comes via arguments made by auteurist critics that a consistency of theme and approach can be detected in Hitchcock's work through different circumstances of production and across a variety of genres. The vitriol directed towards the remake of *Psycho* and its director would appear to stem largely from the feeling that not only is it inferior to the original in almost every way, but it somehow constitutes an injustice to or diminishment of the unique artistic vision of one of Cinema's Great Directors. Thus, Naremore argues that Van Sant committed the sin of copying "not . . . just any film, but . . . the picture that, more than any other, established Hitchcock as the major figure in the auteurist movement and the most influential director in Hollywood history."[6] And Rothman, discussing a change in *mise-en-scène* effected by Van Sant following a dissolve that occurs near the conclusion of the original *Psycho*, complains that he "turns Hitchcock's complex and profound gesture not into a gesture of [his] own, however altered or diminished in meaning and expressiveness that gesture may be. Rather, Van Sant's dissolve is not meaningful or expressive. It does not have the force of a gesture at all."[7]

I, too, much prefer Hitchcock's film to Van Sant's. But so what? I prefer the work of Hitchcock to that of most directors, and the original *Psycho* has always been one of my favorite horror films.[8] It is no crime, nor should it come as a surprise, that Van Sant came up short when placing himself in direct competition against one of the all-time greats. But as an admirer of Van Sant's work over the past fifteen years, I think his *Psycho* warrants, if not the benefit of the doubt, at least a more sympathetic look.

By trying to stop "watching two movies at the same time in [my] mind," so as not to make "quick comparisons constantly," I have begun to see Van Sant's *Psycho* in a different and arguably more interesting light. If a case can be made for Van Sant as an auteur in his own right, someone whose entire body of work evinces a marked consistency at the level of both content and form (better: content through form) despite the existence of significant countervailing forces, then it is possible to read his *Psycho* as the limiting instance of an auteurist text.[9] For what could pose more of a threat to the preservation and furthering of one's artistic vision than attempting a literal remake of another (auteur) director's signature film?

Opening oneself up to the idea that the 1998 *Psycho* is more a "Van Sant film" than a slavish imitation of the original—at best a misconceived homage to Hitchcock— enables one to speculate on what it was about the 1960 version that so attracted Van Sant to it in the first place. And it allows one to interpret the numerous small changes he effected in the remake not simply as facile "updates," or worse, attempted "improvements" on a film that surely does not need improving, but as efforts (perhaps not fully conscious) to make the 1998 *Psycho* his own—to make it cohere that much more with the rest of his work.[10] V.F. Perkins writes that "The connoisseurship implicit in a view of the director as author does not demand that we see a great director's failures as masterpieces, although it may make them more interesting than a feebler artist's successes. By seeing the connections between a director's films we can become more sensitive to the pattern within each of them."[11] Whether or not Van Sant is a great director remains to be seen, and his *Psycho* is no masterpiece. But even if viewed as a failure, the film merits consideration and a degree of credit for the way Van Sant manages to express himself and his worldview, all the while following someone else's blueprint.

In order to establish Van Sant's auteur credentials, we first need to specify what obstacles to the achievement of a singular artistic vision have been present throughout his professional career. The eight feature-length films Van Sant has directed to date have been made under a wide variety of production contexts: *Mala Noche* (1985) was a self-financed black and white arthouse hit, *Drugstore Cowboy* (1989) an award-winning independent, and the remaining six films were made in Hollywood for four different studios with budgets ranging from \$2.5 to \$43 million.[12] *Mala Noche*, *Drugstore Cowboy*, and *My Own Private Idaho* (1991) have all been praised for incorporating elements of both European art cinema (Amy Taubin compares them to Pasolini's films ''in their blend of neo-realism and poetic lyricism'') and American avant-garde ''trance'' cinema.[13] Van Sant's more recent work, however, in particular *Good Will Hunting* (1997) and *Finding Forrester* (2000), is frequently cited as evidence in support of the claim that he has abandoned his experimental/artistic/indie roots for mainstream respectability.[14] Finally, although Van Sant has never made a straightforward genre picture, he regularly employs different generic conventions depending on the film in question. Thus, while *To Die For* (1995) contains elements of both the suspense-thriller and the dark comedy, *Even Cowgirls Get the Blues* (1993) references both the Western and the road movie, and *Finding Forrester* mixes urban drama and the ''odd couple'' buddy picture.

Despite the wide variety of production contexts in which his films have been made, their divergent, possibly contradictory sensibilities, and their pragmatic and playful rather than consistent or committed deployment of hybridized genre conventions, a number of recognizable themes and stylistic signatures can be found throughout Van Sant's entire corpus.[15] All I can do here is make mention of a few of those which seem especially relevant when reconsidering his version of *Psycho*. Above all, one finds in Van Sant's films an interest in rendering the subjective experience of troubled, disaffected youths and young adults. As Rebecca Flint puts it, ''Since debuting . . . with *Mala Noche*, Van Sant has become one of the premiere bards of dysfunction, populating his films with a parade of hustlers, junkies, psychopathic weather girls, and troubled geniuses.''[16] He explores this subjectivity at both the narrative and purely visual levels, frequently incorporating impressionistic (occasionally surrealistic) images or insert shots from what we are to assume is the subject's perspective during moments of heightened experience, e.g., drug highs (*Drugstore Cowboy*), sexual awakenings (*Even Cowgirls Get the Blues*), nostalgic reveries (*My Own Private Idaho*), or traumatic memories (*Good Will Hunting*).

Closely related to this overriding preoccupation are two others: the romantic idea of leaving home and heading on the road in order to escape what are felt to be repressive norms and expectations; and the longing for, and struggle to develop, an intimate relationship (whether primarily sexual, parental, or therapeutic in nature) with another human being. The relationships in question are often between members of the same gender, but homosexuality in his films is never used to make overtly political statements. Other Van Sant signatures include a fascination with restricted vision (e.g., point-of-view shots through binoculars or fingers, highlighted bits of text, iris-outs), the use of first-person voiceover narration, and what can only be described as eccentric casting choices (e.g., the casting of newcomers in lead roles; casting against type; the casting of friends and famous non-actors in bit parts, such as William S. Burroughs and Ken Kesey in *Even Cowgirls Get the Blues*).

How might *Psycho* be read as of a piece with the rest of Van Sant's films, and, going in the other direction, how might a familiarity with Van Sant's signature directorial traits influence a reading of his *Psycho*? At the most basic level, this is a film with two main characters, both of whom are relatively young and more or less dysfunctional (whether socially or psychologically), who engage in impulsive criminal behavior in desperate attempts at satisfying otherwise unattainable desires. Whereas Norman Bates remains rooted to the nowhere in which he was born and raised, Marion Crane gains at least a temporary measure of relief from the restrictive and misogynistic environment in which she lives by getting in her car and driving off shortly after stealing the $400,000 from work. In this respect, she is not unlike the protagonists of Van Sant's other films, who either live on, take to, or fantasize about the road in pursuit of an idealized past (*My Own Private Idaho*, *Finding Forrester*), alternative present (*Mala Noche*, *Drugstore Cowboy*, *Even Cowgirls Get the Blues*), or more promising future (*To Die For*, *Good Will Hunting*).

The impressionistic insert of blue sky and clouds flashing through Marion's mind as she gets stabbed to death in the motel shower metaphorically expresses how important the idea of freedom of movement has become to her. And the fact that Arbogast (William Macy) has a pair of bizarre visions of his own while falling backwards down the stairs of the Bates home at the very least tells us that Van Sant views being murdered as bearing experiential similarities to such altered states of consciousness as orgasm, narcoleptic seizure, and drug-induced hallucination. Subjective experience is again rendered when we are granted interior access to the minds of both Norman and Marion through voiceover narration (Marion while driving, Norman/Mother while sitting in the prison examining room).

It is also worth considering Van Sant's choice of actors. Surely it was no accident that Anne Heche, then at the height of her lesbian infamy, was cast as the perhaps sexually fulfilled but emotionally discontented Marion Crane. Marion's unhappiness stems in large part from her restricted position in a society where men either presume or assume a measure of control over her mind and body. As Thomas Hemmeter notes, "the cramped spaces of this person's life reflect her desperate social situation, a single woman in an unfulfilling job, without the financial resources to do what the culture demanded of women in this period: to get married."[17] By seeing through this character to the actress who plays her, Van Sant's viewers are encouraged to suspect that a radical change in lifestyle may be just what the doctor ordered, a way out of the "private trap" that Marion mistakenly believes she stepped into only when committing her crime.

Hitchcock's calculated casting of Anthony Perkins as Norman Bates in the original *Psycho* capitalized on the fact that it was, if not well known, at least widely suspected that Perkins was gay, and the manhood of his persona on screen was often questioned (e.g., *Fear Strikes Out*, 1957). This extra-textual data enabled Hitchcock to partially circumvent the era's restrictive production codes while providing additional support for an interpretation of Norman as homosexual. Although Van Sant's *Psycho* revisits Hitchcock's exaggerated "butt shot" from below of Norman walking up the stairs, and despite Vince Vaughn's somewhat effeminate portrayal, the decision to cast this physically imposing, six-foot-five-inch leading-man type—one whose resolutely macho heterosexual identity was well-established from previous films (e.g., *Swingers*, 1996)—in the role of Norman can be seen as a distinctively Van Santian casting against expectation (cf. *Naked Lunch* author William S. Burroughs as the not-so-recovered drug addict and priest Father Tom in *Drugstore Cowboy*). Van Sant's surprising and frequently criticized decision to have Norman masturbate to a peephole view of Marion stripping down in the bathroom (an example of restricted vision) may just have been a not-too-subtle means of reinforcing his heterosexual orientation in contrast to Perkins, who in the equivalent scene merely stares at Marion ineffectually.

Following this line of thought, it is at least plausible that Norman's murder of Marion is motivated not so much by his dead mother's imagined jealousy as by his own rage at Marion's (possibly lesbian) indifference to his heterosexual and possessive male gaze. Finally, Julianne Moore's portrayal of Lila Crane as more "butch" and independent than both her sister and her counterpart, Vera Miles, in the original *Psycho*—she even participates in the capture of Norman by giving him a swift kick—makes her representative of a more liberated order of woman, reminiscent of lesbian cowgirl

Bonanza Jellybean (Rain Phoenix) in *Even Cowgirls Get the Blues*.[18]

I have not bothered to separate out the Hitchcock from the Van Sant in this brief and admittedly sketchy auteurist reading of the 1998 *Psycho*. I think that such an exercise, while it may be entertaining, is ultimately of limited interest. What makes *Psycho* a Hitchcock film is that, as numerous critics and scholars have argued, it manifests the authorial control and artistic trademarks evident throughout Hitchcock's entire corpus, across a wide variety of production contexts and generic frameworks. What makes the remake a Van Sant film, regardless of its enormous and transparent debt to the original, is that it succeeds in finding ways to cohere, both thematically and stylistically, with the rest of its director's recognizable though diverse body of work. In the case of Van Sant's *Psycho*, the auteur became a provoca(u)teur.

Notes

1. Philip Baker Hall (Sheriff Al Chambers in the remake), interviewed in *Psycho Path*, the "Making of" documentary accompanying Universal's DVD release of Gus Van Sant's *Psycho*.

2. "Gus Comes Clean," online interview with Gus Van Sant, http://www.monk.com (October 1998).

3. William Rothman, "Some Thoughts on Hitchcock's Authorship," in *Alfred Hitchcock: Centenary Essays*, ed. Richard Allen and S. Ishii-Gonzalès (London: BFI, 1999), 29.

4. James Naremore, "Remaking *Psycho*," *Hitchcock Annual* (1999-2000), 4.

5. Esther Anatolitis, "Re-making the remake: Gus Van Sant's *Psycho*," *Toto: Cinema Matters*, http://www.cse.unsw.edu.au/~peteg/toto/psycho.htm.

6. Naremore, "Remaking *Psycho*," 5-6.

7. Rothman, "Some Thoughts on Hitchcock's Authorship," 33.

8. I beg to differ with Naremore's claim that "For all its continuing interest, *Psycho* is no longer a cutting-edge horror film. Hitchcock's dark satire of American sex and money has entered into popular folklore and become part of the cinema's imaginary museum, but it is also of its time and place" (12). For an essay arguing that (and

why) the three manifest horror scenes in *Psycho* do not lose their impact even upon repeated viewings, see my "Manufacturing Horror in Hitchcock's *Psycho*," *CineAction* 50 (October 1999), 70-75.

9. My understanding of auteur theory is indebted to a graduate seminar taught by Thomas Elsaesser at New York University in the Spring of 2001.

10. In *Psycho Path*, the Russian director Andrei Konchalovsky responds as follows to an interviewer's question whether Van Sant can be seen as having attempted a "forgery" of Hitchcock's film: "The forger doesn't want to be found. This thing is signed. Signed by Gus Van Sant. It's reproducing something and saying look at it, I did it, not him."

11. V.F. Perkins, *Film as Film: Understanding and Judging Movies* (New York: Penguin, 1986), 186.

12. Van Sant has also directed a number of quality shorts and music videos.

13. Amy Taubin, "Objects of Desire," *Sight and Sound* (January 1992), rpt. in *American Independent Cinema: A* Sight and Sound *Reader,* ed. Jim Hillier (London: BFI, 2001), 79.

14. Arguably, this is as much a snobbish reaction to the commercial success of these latter films as a negative judgment regarding their relatively linear narratives and unobtrusive visuals.

15. For example, while a number of Van Sant's films are adaptations from novels (*Mala Noche, Drugstore Cowboy, Even Cowgirls Get the Blues, To Die For*), two of them are original screenplays by then-Hollywood newcomers (*Good Will Hunting, Finding Forrester*), and one he wrote the script for himself (*My Own Private Idaho*).

16. Rebecca Flint, *All Movie Guide*, http://www.allmovie.com/cg/avg.dll.

17. Thomas Hemmeter, "Horror Beyond the Camera: Cultural Sources of Violence in Hitchcock's Mid-Century America," forthcoming in *Post Script: Essays in Film and the Humanities*, special issue on "Realist Horror Cinema."

18. Parts of this paragraph are taken from my essay, "A Tale of Two *Psycho*s (Prelude to a Future Reassessment)," in the online journal *Senses of Cinema* 10 (November 2000), http://www.sensesofcinema.com/contents/00/10/psychos.html. A huge assist goes to Bruce La Bruce for sharing his thoughts with me via e-mail about Van Sant's casting of Marion and Norman. Sincerest thanks to Richard Allen, Bruce La Bruce, and Sidney Gottlieb for their helpful comments, questions, and criticisms of an earlier version of the present essay.

AN ANALYSIS OF THE PARLOR SCENE IN *PSYCHO* X 2

SAM ISHII-GONZALÈS

My objective here is quite simple. By comparing the parlor scene in the two versions of *Psycho* I will demonstrate how alterations made to the original structure in the "shot-by-shot" remake manage to divest this sequence not only of its emotional intensity and its thematic resonance but also of Hitchcock.

Let me begin with a summary of the parlor scene as it appears in the original.[1] This nine-minute scene takes place thirty-five minutes into the film and shortly after Marion, caught in a rainstorm, finds shelter at the Bates Motel. Norman, having been chastised by his mother for inviting strange women to dinner, appears at Marion's motel room door with a tray of food. He suggests that they have their meal in the parlor behind his office. The first seven shots of this sequence are "classical" in their delineation of cinematic space and figural placement. It is with the eighth shot—which coincides with Norman's words "You—you eat like a bird"—that Hitchcock reveals the scene's dominant structural form: the shot/reverse shot (S/RS). In other words, the meaning of this encounter between Norman and Marion will be established by Hitchcock through the rhythmic alternation of two faces, two beings, viewed in isolation. (From this point onward there will only be two more occasions in which Norman and Marion will be seen together within the frame, each an inversion of the other: Norman's silhouette advancing upon Marion as she showers; Marion's shrouded corpse carried by Norman out of the bathroom.)

There are four S/RS series in total in this scene and each series introduces a new framing of the two characters.

Series A: Norman in medium shot (MS), slightly off-center to the right of the frame; Marion in a MS, slightly off to the left.

Series B: Norman in low-angle medium profile shot with a stuffed owl hovering on the upper left hand corner of the frame; Marion in a more tightly framed MS.

Series C: Norman in a medium close-up (MCU) with a stuffed black bird prominent on the table to his right; Marion in MCU, abstracted from her immediate surroundings.[2]

Series D: Norman in a high-angle MS; Marion (who rises to leave at the beginning of this series) in a MS with a stuffed black raven appearing to her left.

The use of S/RS as a means of organizing a dialogue sequence is not unusual. Indeed, it is a classical form of *découpage*. But what is atypical and distinctive about the series of shot/reverse shots in Hitchcock's *Psycho* is the rigidity and relentlessness with which the filmmaker presents them, one immediately following the other. Series A repeats forty times without variation, followed by series B, which repeats twenty-eight times without variation, series C, which repeats nineteen times without variation, and series D, which repeats twelve times without variation. The structural center of this sequence thus consists of four individual shots each of Norman and Marion which alternate and repeat ninety-nine times in strict succession. (The sequence as a whole contains one-hundred-and-nine shots.)

Why does Hitchcock do this? To answer this question we must clarify the specific points in Marion and Norman's conversation that occasion a shift from one series to the next. Series A concludes with Marion's ''You know, if anyone ever talked to me the way I heard—the way she spoke to you.'' The countershot of Norman, half way through Marion's comment, begins series B. Series B ends with Marion's ''Wouldn't it better—if you put her—someplace?'' The conclusion of series C alters the previously established pattern of even numbered S/RS blocks on a shot of Norman suggesting to Marion that she personalize her impersonal gratitude. ''Thank You, Norman,'' he says, wishing to continue or extend their intimacy. The shift in rhythm here—from even to odd, from the series beginning with Norman to the series beginning with Marion—suggests that the final dozen shots represent Marion's attempt to free herself from this intimacy, to extract herself from his presence and regain a sense of equilibrium. It also makes clear that the first three series (eighty-seven shots in total) belong to Norman. In other words, it is the subtle shifts of emotion that Norman experiences as he speaks with Marion that are conveyed through the *découpage* and the *mise-en-scène*. It is thus no mere accident that the transition from one series to the next coincides with Marion's references to his mother. What Hitchcock wishes to convey here, I would suggest, is the precarious mental state of his character Norman Bates. And he does so not through the use of point-of-view shots or the simulation of Norman Bates's perspectival subjectivity but through the fixity and solitude of these extended S/RS passages.[3] This fixity is interrupted only by the imposition of "mother" or by the attempts of others—in this case, Marion—to withdraw from his desolate world, his "private trap."

Now let's turn to the parlor scene in Van Sant's remake, specifically his handling of the four S/RS series. Although the framing of the characters in series A is roughly comparable in both versions, Van Sant starts his analytic breakdown not with a shot of Norman saying "You—you eat like a bird" but with a silent shot of Marion as she begins to eat. This S/RS series, having already begun on a different note, then manages to repeat only four times before there is an interruption in the form of an insert shot: a detail of one of Norman's stuffed birds (motivated as a point-of-view shot from his viewpoint and by the line "My hobby is stuffing things—you know: taxidermy"). Van Sant not only alters the rhythmic structure of Hitchcock's but he does so in order to introduce a shot that the latter expressly avoids, a shot exterior to the intersubjective drama that is unfolding. In Hitchcock, the characters look offscreen but we remain focused exclusively on them.

This is merely the first of several deviations from the original structure which Van Sant introduces. The most incomprehensible is his use of camera movements to reframe Norman immediately prior to the line of dialogue that, in Hitchcock, marks a shift from one series to the next. So that instead of introducing a new framing of Norman when Marion says "the way she spoke to you . . ." Van Sant's camera dollies around Norman as Marion says, "You know, if anyone ever talked to me the way I heard . . ." until he is repositioned in the frame. In other words, his camera telegraphs a shift in their relations before it has actually taken place. Van Sant does this again at then end of series B. The camera repositions Norman as he says "You understand that I don't hate her—I hate what she has become," before Marion has even suggested that it might be better to put her "someplace"! Van Sant thus undermines the very purpose of Hitchcock's strict regime of S/RS and at the precise moments they yield their meaning. In neither case, I might add, does Van Sant use this reframing to mark a shift in Norman's relations with Marion. Instead, he follows this new view of Norman with a return to Marion still framed as she was in the previous series. The new S/RS series begins only after a momentary delay or hiccup, the effect of which is to render arbitrary, even pointless what was once stunningly exact.

The framing of Norman in series C is another inexplicable modification. Van Sant—having added a long-tailed green bird to the clutter of Marion's series of shots—eliminates the presence of a stuffed black bird that appears to Norman's right. (The bird is seen in the wider shot that begins the series but even here it is positioned differently than in the original, facing away from Norman instead of towards him.) Hitchcock uses this composition to produce a disturbing mirror effect: the framing of Norman in series A is reproduced in the framing of Marion in series D. The stuffed black bird to Norman's right—whose beak appears at one point (as he menacingly leans forward) to be within millimeters of his face—becomes, in series D, a stuffed raven to Marion's left, its beak within millimeters of her face. This mirror image strikes a new chord on the motif of doubling and uncanny replication that haunts the film.[4] It also indicates what the shower sequence will shortly confirm: Marion will not succeed in removing herself from Norman's gaze (and vice versa); she has found her place in his world.[5]

The parlor scene beautifully affirms Hitchcock's axiom that it is through "purely cinematic means"—i.e., through *mise-en-scène* and montage—that subject matter gains its meaning. As Rohmer and Chabrol once claimed, "In Hitchcock's work form does not embellish content, it creates it."[6] Form is not added to meaning that is preexistent. Meaning is discovered in the elaboration of form. This, for Hitchcock, was the power of "pure cinema," and it is precisely in this sense that Van Sant fails to make (or remake) a Hitchcock film. That he does not comprehend this (listen, for instance, to the audio commentary on the DVD collector's edition of his *Psycho*) is perhaps the saddest thing of all—sadder even than the film itself.

Notes

I would like to thank the students in Practical Film Analysis at the Film/Media Department at Hunter College for their enthusiasm and critical engagement with my semester-long study of Hitchcock's work.

1. For another analysis of this sequence (and one which usefully includes frame enlargements of all the relevant shots), see William Rothman, "*Psycho*," in *Hitchcock—The Murderous Gaze* (Cambridge: Harvard University Press, 1982), 279-88.

2. As Rothman points out, the shots in series B and C increasingly sever Marion from the objective setting of the Bates parlor. In series B, we can still see the bottom half of the oval painting on the wall behind her, a section of the couch she sits upon, the mouth of the milk jug sitting on the table, a part of the window curtain to Marion's left side; in series C, all that is left is the very bottom of the painting and the upper half of the sofa chair, both of which register (in black-and-white) as nearly abstract graphic markings. See *The Murderous Gaze*, 283-85.

3. As George Toles points out in his brilliant analysis of the film, the scene between Marion and Norman perversely duplicates

the meeting between Marion and Sam at the beginning of the film. Indeed, Toles argues that the shot/reverse shots which Hitchcock uses for Norman and Marion are a form of mirror reflection. Describing the scenes at the registration desk and in cabin one that precede the parlor conversation, he writes, "In Hitchcock's shot-countershot cutting between Norman and Marion, we notice the profile views of the two facing figures are perfectly symmetrical. Norman occupies the extreme right-hand side of an imbalanced frame, Marion the extreme left-hand side in alternate shots: mirror images." See " 'If Thine Eye Offend Thee . . .': *Psycho* and the Art of Infection," in Richard Allen and S. Ishii-Gonzalès eds., *Alfred Hitchcock: Centenary Essays* (London: BFI, 1999), 167.

4. The significance of mirrors to Hitchcock's conception of the film is vouched by screenwriter Joseph Stefano in a discussion with Janet Leigh: "He mentioned something about mirrors . . . Then he mentioned them again later on. It was so typical of Hitchcock that if he liked something visually he wanted to do it more," qtd. in Bill Krohn, *Hitchcock at Work* (London: Phaidon, 2000), 221.

5. For Norman, Marion's place in his world is affirmed by two "facts" that come out during their final exchange: the knowledge that she has lied about her name—which reveals her shared propensity for secrecy or deceptiveness (and in the guise of two identities: Marie Samuels and Marion Crane)—and, of course, her surname which links Marion to his hobby which is more-than-a-hobby ("I think only birds look well stuffed").

6. Eric Rohmer and Claude Chabrol, *Hitchcock: The First Forty-Four Films*, trans. Stanley Hochman (New York: Frederick Ungar, 1979), 152; originally published in French in 1957.

PSYCHO (REDUX)

CONSTANTINE VEREVIS

Much of the talk leading up to and following the release of Gus Van Sant's 1998 remake—or "replica"—of the Alfred Hitchcock film *Psycho* (1960) was an expression of outrage and confusion at the defilement of a beloved classic. For instance, and most prominently, the "*Psycho*: Saving a Classic" web-site described the remake as a "disgrace" and urged members to boycott the opening weekend.[1] Reviewers and Hitchcockians alike agreed that Van Sant made two fundamental mistakes: the first was to have undertaken to remake a landmark of cinematic history, and the second was to have followed the Hitchcock original (almost) shot by shot, line by line. As the reviewer for the *New York Post* remarked, "If you're going to be hubristic enough to remake *Psycho*, you should at least have the courage to put your own spin on it."[2] But even for those who noted that the shooting script for the remake was only about ninety percent the same as Hitchcock's, Van Sant's revisions were thought to have added nothing to what remained, for them, an intact and undeniable classic, a semantic fixity against which the new version was evaluated and dismissed as a degraded copy.[3] For these fans and critics—for these reviewers—the *Psycho* remake was ultimately nothing more than a blatant rip-off: not only an attempt to exploit the original film's legendary status, but (worse) a cheap imitation of one of the "best and best known of American films."[4]

A modern classic, *Psycho* has been retrospectively coded as the forerunner to the cycle of slasher movies of the 1970s and beyond initiated by *Halloween*, and celebrated in the sequels and series that followed: notably, *Halloween II-V* and *H20*, but also *A Nightmare on Elm Street I-V* and *Friday the 13th, Parts I-VIII* (plus *Jason Goes to Hell: The Final Friday*). In this cycle, *Psycho* is the benchmark, with Marion Crane as the "first girl" (the beautiful, sexually active victim); her sister, Lila, as the first "final girl" (the survivor); and, of course,

Norman Bates as the original "psycho."[5] The late seventies' interest in the slasher movie sub-genre, coupled with the burgeoning home-video market of the early 1980s, led to the revival of the character of Norman Bates for *Psycho II* (Richard Franklin, 1983), a sequel in which Norman (played again by Anthony Perkins) returns to the Bates Motel after twenty-two years in a mental institution. This was followed by two further sequels (both featuring Perkins): *Psycho III* (directed by Anthony Perkins, 1986), which picks up from the narrative twist (introduced at the end of part II) that Mrs Bates was Norman's adoptive mother; and *Psycho IV: The Beginning* (Mick Garris, 1990), which functions (through the use of numerous flashbacks) as a kind of "prequel" to the 1960 film. Additionally, there was *Bates Motel* (Richard Rothstein, 1987), an unsuccessful television feature and pilot for a proposed television series, in which Norman hands over management of the motel to a fellow mental hospital inmate (played by Bud Cort).

Curiously, few (if any) of the commentaries at the time of the release of Van Sant's *Psycho* drew attention to this cycle of 1980s *Psycho* films, even though each of its constituent parts might be understood as a kind of "limited remake" of the Hitchcock original. For instance, *Psycho II* begins with a shot of the Bates Motel neon sign (showing a vacancy) followed by a replaying of the original *Psycho*'s shower sequence, almost in its entirety. The film then goes on to carefully remake not only aspects of that sequence (and its lead up), but also such shots as the silhouetted *Psycho* house, the overhead view of Norman carrying his invalid mother to the cellar, and even a suitcase tumbling backwards down the stairs in imitation of Arbogast's body. In these instances, as well as in *Psycho III* and *IV* and a host of Hitchcock homages and parodies—from the films of Brian De Palma (notably, *Dressed to Kill*, 1980) to Mel Brooks's *High Anxiety* (1977)—allusion to particular shots and sequences can be understood as a limited form of remaking, a type of "citation effect," or "iterability, that exists in and for every film."[6] These examples suggest that the precursor text is never singular, and that Van Sant's *Psycho* remake differs textually (from this cycle of films) not in kind, but only in degree. Its status as recognized (and recognizable) remake, as well as the valorization of the Hitchcock original as an unchanging essence, is better attributed to broader institutional factors. These would include, as evinced in the aforementioned reviews, such things as authorship, film literacy, and canon formation, which have led to Hitchcock becoming a special example to filmmakers and reviewers alike.[7]

While the above approach establishes a much broader circuit between the 1960 and the 1998 *Psycho* than that accorded by most of its reviewers, there is another, perhaps more interesting position: namely, that Van Sant's *Psycho* is not close enough to the Hitchcock version. Roger Ebert explains: "Curious, how similar the new version is, and how different. . . . The movie is an invaluable experiment in the theory of cinema, because it demonstrates that a shot-by-shot remake is pointless; genius apparently resides between or beneath the shots."[8] This suggestion—that an irreducible difference plays simultaneously between the most mechanical of repetitions—is best demonstrated by an earlier (and lesser known) remake of *Psycho*, Douglas Gordon's *24 Hour Psycho* (1993).[9] So named because it takes twenty-four hours to run its course, Gordon's version is a video installation piece that reruns Hitchcock's *Psycho* at approximately two frames per second, just fast enough for each image to be pulled forward into the next. Drawing upon the formal precedents of the North American "structural" film (notably Ken Jacob's *Tom, Tom, the Piper's Son* [1969]), Gordon's strategy demonstrates that each and every film is remade—i.e., dispersed and transformed—in its every new context or configuration. Accordingly, Gordon does not set out to imitate *Psycho* but to repeat it—that is, to change nothing, but at the same time allow an absolute difference to emerge. Understood in this way, Van Sant's *Psycho* might be thought of not as a perversion of an original identity, but as the production of a new event, one that adds to (rather than corrupts) the seriality of the former version. If Hitchcock's work holds for its viewers some ongoing fascination, then it is perhaps because these viewers remake the work in its every reviewing, and this reviewing may be no more or less than the genre labelled "remake."

Notes

1. *"Psycho:* Saving a Classic," http://members.aol.com/montag17/psycho.html.
2. See Reviews, http://members.aol.com/montag17/psycho.html (February 12, 1999).
3. John Harkness, *"Psycho* Path," http://www.now.com (February 12, 1999).
4. A number of commentaries, including "Saving a Classic" and the official web-site (http://www.psychomovie.com), made a point of noting that *Psycho* was ranked number 18 in the American Film Institute's centenary list of the 100 most important American movies.
5. For a concise discussion of *Psycho* as prototype of the slasher movie, see Carol J. Clover, "Her Body, Himself: Gender in the Slasher Film," in James Donald, ed., *Fantasy and the Cinema* (London: BFI, 1989), 91-133.
6. David Wills, "The French Remark: *Breathless* and Cinematic Citationality," in Andrew Horton and Stuart Y. McDougal, eds., *Play It Again, Sam: Retakes on Remakes* (Berkeley: University of California Press, 1998), 148.
7. With respect the canonization of the work of Alfred Hitchcock, see Robert P. Kolker, "Algebraic Figures: Recalculating the Hitchcock Formula," in Horton and McDougal, eds., *Play It Again, Sam,* 34-51.
8. RogerEbert,http://members.aol.com/montag17/psycho.html (February 12, 1999).
9. *24 Hour Psycho* most recently toured as part of the Alfred Hitchcock centenary exhibition, *Notorious.* See the exhibition catalogue, *Notorious: Alfred Hitchcock and Contemporary Art* (Oxford: Museum of Contemporary Art, 1999).

Book Reviews

Guy Cogeval and Dominique Paini, ed., *Hitchcock and Art: Fatal Coincidences*. Montreal: Montreal Museum of Fine Arts/ Milan: Edizioni Gabriele Mazzotta, 2000. 498 pp. $25 paper.

MARSHALL DEUTELBAUM

Hitchcock's films are now so central an inspiration and source of imagery for contemporary British artists that it is difficult to imagine how the English film journal *Sequence* might have been so dismissive of his American films as to declare in 1947 that *"Spellbound* and *Notorious* [are] classic examples of brilliance run to seed, . . . heartless and soulless ingenuity."[1] The shift in English esteem for Hitchcock's American films over the intervening years can be seen in how the titles of the very films scorned by *Sequence* have been used as titles for recent English exhibitions illustrating the centrality of popular film in general and Hitchcock's films in particular for artists working in a variety of media.

Spellbound: Art and Film, the Hayward Gallery's 1996 exhibition, for example, included Douglas Gordon's installation, *24 Hour Psycho*, in which the film's projection at two frames per second stretches its narrative out over an entire day. Shown this way, Amy Taubin notes,

> the film retains just enough motion for us to feel how each image is pulled towards the next. No matter how slowly the wheels grind, the end *will* come. And at the end lies nullification, which is worse than death.[2]

More recently, the Museum of Modern Art at Oxford mounted *Notorious: Alfred Hitchcock and Contemporary Art*, an exhibition showing the uses of Hitchcock's works by thirteen artists. Among the works included were Cindy Sherman's photographs, an excerpt from *San Soleil* (Chris Marker's 16mm meditation on *Vertigo's* San Francisco), and Stan Douglas' 16mm loop film, *Subject to a Film: Marnie*.[3]

Writing in the Foreword to the catalogue of the Oxford show, Kerry Brougher describes how these appropriations of Hitchcockian imagery unavoidably strip the images of their original meanings and encourage an entirely different response. Much as Taubin described the effect of *Psycho's* slowed projection, Brougher notes that such

> reframing of film has the effect of negating the original power of cinema to suspend disbelief and in its place creating a meditation on the nature of cinema and the way film language operates. Rather than watching film we begin to watch ourselves watching. (4)

Whereas the previous exhibitions mentioned above traced the direct indebtedness of contemporary artists to Hitchcock's imagery, *Hitchcock and Art: Fatal Coincidences* approaches Hitchcock and his films from the opposite direction, more allusively suggesting how artistic currents during the director's formative years can be seen to have manifested themselves in Hitchcock's recurrent themes and directorial signature.

The exhibition and its dense, richly illustrated catalogue by co-curators Guy Cogeval, director of the Montreal Museum of Fine Arts, and Dominique Paini, director of the Cinémathèque Francaise, seek to suggest, through the juxtaposition of art works with images from Hitchcock's films, the shared affinities between the director's visual sensibilities and the dominant aesthetics around him. In the opening essay, appropriately entitled "Associations, Constellations, Likenesses, Construction," Paini cautions the reader not to expect certainties because

> Hitchcock is not so much exhibited here as "dreamt," through the *associations* that the sleep state

encourages—or perhaps "authorizes" is the better term. . . .

We have placed our trust in intuitive *constellations* of images that stood out upon seeing the films again. (19)

Cogeval and Paini offer not direct influences, then, but suggestive, echoing coincidences they have discerned (though never fatal, despite the catalogue's title!). Thus the exhibition is more a triumph of their ability to make connections between art works than an interpretive explanation of the sources of Hitchcock's imagery. They adroitly justify their approach by claiming that their exhibition's allusive order mimics Hitchcock's own method. Cogeval neatly aligns their method with what they purport to be Hitchcock's:

The Hitchcock approach is not literal; it is not about composing images as one would a painting. . . . It would be more accurate to say that Hitchcock—and this is what is most striking in this exhibition— engages in a subtle, sometimes clandestine reactivation of Victorian, Decadent and Symbolist culture of the late 19th century, via a sort of ultimate, nostalgic, salvationist reflex, which is understandable for an auteur who was British and Catholic. (22-23)

The exhibited works fill the latter half of the catalogue, their layout on the page as important to the curators' argument as any essay in the book.[4]

The first half of the catalogue consists of eighteen essays, including the initial pair in which Cogeval and Paini explain their aims. Curiously, few of the essays mention art at all. And even when Hitchcock's work is tied to art, the result is often disappointing, either because the terms that film and painting share are used so casually, or because the analysis is freighted with more allusive significance than the cinematic reference can bear. The following passage from Jean-Louis Schefer's "Hitchcock's Female Portraits," for example,

illustrates the fluctuating meaning of the word "portrait"—
the word appearing both with and without quotes—as
something painted, something ideational, or sometimes even
something corporeal:

> Scenes where "portraits" are being cleaned or
> restored are essential to Hitchcock's films, for one
> element in the story must remain unchanged, secure.
> That element is the beloved one, the woman whose
> image is conjured up in dreams (the living portrait in
> *Vertigo*, Lady Flusky in *Under Capricorn*, and many
> more). Unlike Byzantine icons, this image is not the
> object of cult worship, nor is it repainted when the
> occasion requires. The image is closely guarded,
> however, becoming the object often of almost fatal
> devotion; this is so in all of Hitchcock's films, including
> the extraordinary *Shadow of a Doubt*, in which the young
> Charlie Newton lives for and suffers by the idealized
> portrait of her uncle, played by Joseph Cotten. (108)

The mention of "Byzantine icons" further accentuates the
slipperiness of meaning, since Schefer begins his essay by
declaring the films indebtedness to quite a different medium:
"Hitchcock's *oeuvre* resembles classic pastel compositions in
its choice of subjects, attention to detail (the sheen on eyes,
hands, and skin), colour and quality of lighting and
materials" (101).

A few pages later, a passage in Alain Bergala's "Alfred,
Adam and Eve" illustrates how the suggestion of art historical antecedents for the recurrent scene in Hitchcock's films
of a couple arguing on a hilltop can approach overkill.
Beginning by declaring these scenes "reminiscent of 15th-
century Italian paintings of Adam and Eve being chased from
the Garden of Eden," Bergala then contends that these
scenes look different from other scenes in the films:

> Compared to the rest of the film, this image always
> looks "primitive," matching the figurative innocence

and simplicity that marked the beginning of the quattrocentro style. Hitchcock deliberately uses artificial-looking props (transplanted trees, for instance) to recreate a "naïve" landscape—one is reminded of the "cardboard" rocks of Giotto. Eden, for him, is not an Akkadian [*sic*] "plain" or a Sumerian "fertile ground"; rather, it is a small, fairly arid hill, covered by only a few spindly trees or hedges. Fra Angelico's *Annunciation* altarpieces at Cortona offers the closest model for these stylized studio landscapes in which a man and woman, outlined against the sky, confront one another. (116)

Happily, there are other, more rewarding essays in the collection. Julia Tanski's excellent "The Symbolist Woman in Alfred Hitchcock's Films" and Stephane Aquin's "Hitchcock and Contemporary Art" are well written and insightful. In addition, there are two essays on Hitchcock's collaboration with Salvador Dali for the surreal dream sequence in *Spellbound*. In "Such Stuff as Dreams are Made On: Hitchcock and Dali, Surrealism and Oneiricism," Nathalie Bondil-Poupard traces not only the history of that famous sequence from its inception through to its emasculation by David O. Selznick, but also details Hitchcock's own use of dreams and dream material in his other films. Her essay is supplemented by "Hitchcock and Dali: The Lost Dreams of *Spellbound*," which includes the dialogue originally written for the dream sequence and a fascinating collection of sketches and production photographs, including several of Ingrid Bergman's transformation.

Cogeval and Paini arrange the art works themselves by thematic category. "Yet Each Man Kills the Thing He Loves (Oscar Wilde)," for example, arranges paintings by Dante Gabriele Rossetti and Edward Burne-Jones alongside photographs by Julia Margaret Cameron and stills of Ingrid Bergman in *Under Capricorn* to suggest Hitchcock's indebtedness to the representation of Victorian women. Mortality enters via images of voyeurism, particularly through the juxtaposition of Odeon Redon's rendering of eyes with the images from *Psycho* of Norman's peering eye and the superimposition of Marion's lifeless open eye and the shower drain. The swirl of water in that drain is echoed by the body caught in a similar swirl in Gaetano Previati's *A Descent into the Maelstrom* (1890). This is followed, in turn, by images of floating women—including such familiar images as Madeleine in San Francisco Bay and Millais' *Study for Ophelia* (1852), as well as by a pair of lesser known though equally haunting works by Fernand Khnopff from the 1890s and Willy Schlobach's painting *The Dead Woman* (1890).

While the art works and images from Hitchcock's films frequently echo one another's subjects, Cogeval and Paini are equally sensitive to graphic parallels. For example, the opening in the rocks through which a figure can be seen standing on a beach in a still from *The Manxman* is juxtaposed with an oil painting by Maurice Denis, *The Solitude of Christ* (1918). Both images present a rocky shore, but more intriguingly, the opening in the rock in the film still is very nearly a perfect outline of the painted figure of Christ kneeling in prayer. Here, as elsewhere, the curators demonstrate their keen sense of visual parallels. Thus the crowd on a sidewalk in a still from *Sabotage* seems merely superficially similar to the crowd of pedestrians in George Grosz's painting, *Kurfürstendam* (1925), until one notices that the hat, facial expression, and pointed nose of a man's profile in the still closely resemble the same features of the profile of the man who dominates the painting.

Not surprisingly, this sort of play of similarities is most evident in the section labeled "Forms and Rhythms," which begins by juxtaposing iron grillwork in stills from four of Hitchcock's films with Gustave Caillebotte's painting *The Balcony* (1890), in which similarly shaped grillwork nearly obscures the view of the street below. In the same way, images of parallel lines created by cast shadows and superimpositions in stills from four films are juxtaposed with Paul Klee's painting *Captive (Figure of This World/Next World)* (1940), constructed largely of crosshatched lines that might be read as a similar pattern. The comparison between the deeply carved parallel grooves in the face of Mount Rushmore in a still from *North by Northwest* with the close parallel lines in Paul Klee's *Rock Temple* (1925) continues this pattern, though less convincingly.

As striking as these formal similarities are, because the comparisons are so unmotivated they reveal more about the curators' connoisseurship than about Hitchcock's films. A quintet of images involving trains and converging lines illustrates why such eye-catching patterns are intriguing but uninformative. Charles Borup's photograph of train tracks, a low-angle shot of train tracks and switches from *Strangers on a Train*, Alfred Junge's sketch of a train yard for *Young and Innocent*, and a still from *Shadow of a Doubt* of Uncle Charlie falling in front of an onrushing train on one page are placed beside a full-page reproduction of Ralston Crawford's painting, *Lights in an Aircraft Plant* (1945). All that connects these images is the familiar sense of railroad tracks converging at a great distance in the background. Because Cogeval and Paini are only interested in graphic similarities, it makes no difference that the converging lines in Crawford's painting are rows of industrial lights near the top of the painting, not railroad tracks. Cogeval and Paini might better have compared Ralston's painting with a still from *Saboteur* illustrating the same graphic pattern created by ranks of ceiling lights seen through the open doors of an aircraft plant at the beginning of the film. For an image of railroad tracks converging in the distance, a better comparison for this trope with a painting by Ralston Crawford would be his *At The Dock* (1942), in which railroad tracks at the bottom of the canvas rather than overhead light fixtures meet in deep perspective.[5]

If I find these similar images intriguing but largely unconvincing, it is because the curators have built their exhibition on the comparison of single frame from Hitchcock's films with images that are entire works. As illustrated by my suggestion above about what a more appropriate painting by Ralston Crawford might be, not only is this game of comparisons arbitrary, it is unavoidably unequal because Hitchcock's visual art derives from the flow of images, not from any single image. Out of context, a single frame from a film may be "artistic," but without the images that surround it, it no longer has much meaning. In this regard it may be worth pointing out Natalie Bondil-Poupard's error in claiming that "Hitchcock drew on the montage aesthetic of Slav[k]o Vorkapich." in developing the shifting meaning of the portrait of the laughing harlequin in Blackmail (182). More accurately, the editing involving the painting—its juxtaposition with the shots around it—illustrates the Kuleshov effect, which demonstrated how the meaning of an unchanging image changes as its contexts, the images with which it is juxtaposed, change. This function of cinematic juxtaposition is far different from the juxtapositions on which this exhibition is based. Thus I recommend Hitchcock and Art: Fatal Coincidences less for what it reveals about Hitchcock's artistry than for how much it can sharpen one's visual perception. For just as L.B. Jefferies teaches Lisa and Stella the value of careful, comparative visual analysis in Rear Window, a patient, comparative study of the images in Hitchcock and Art: Fatal Coincidences can help readers to see Hitchcock's films with a heightened sensitivity to their frequent play of the visual analogy so central to Hitchcock's art.

Notes

1. As quoted by Thomas Elsaesser in "Two Decades in Another Country: Hollywood and the Cinephiles," in Superculture: American Popular Culture and Europe, ed. C.W.E. Bigsby (London: Paul Elek, 1975), 201.

2. Amy Taubin, "Douglas Gordon," Spellbound: Art and Film, ed. Phillip Dodd and Ian Christie (London: Hayward Gallery/BFI Publishing, 1996), 69.

3. Notorious: Alfred Hitchcock and Contemporary Art (Oxford: Museum of Modern Art, 1999). Also worth noting is Chris Marker's interactive CD-ROM, Immemory (1997), in which he wittily conflates his memories of Vertigo's Madeleine with the effects of Proust's

madeleine. Originally an installation at the *Centre Georges Pompidou* in Paris, *Immemory* was published by *Editions du Centre Pompidou* in 1998. In 1997, the museum also published *Qu'est-ce qu'une Madeleine?*, a pair of essays (in French and English) by Laurent Roth and Raymond Bellour offering a gloss on *Immemory*. Hitchcock's films, especially *Vertigo*, figure prominently in the exhibition, *Art and Film Since 1945: Hall of Mirrors*, organized in 1996 by Kerry Brougher for the Museum of Contemporary Art, Los Angeles. For essays accompanying the exhibition, see Kerry Brougher, *Art and Film Since 1945: Hall of Mirrors* (Los Angeles and New York: Museum of Contemporary Art, Los Angeles and the Monacelli Press, 1996).

4. For illustrations of the museum installation and a review of the exhibition by an art historian, see Sue Taylor, "The Man Who Saw Too Much," *Art in America* (June, 2001): 36-39, 41.

5. See William C. Agee, *Ralston Crawford: Painting and Visual Experience* (Pasadena, CA: Twelve Trees Press, 1983), plate 20.

Steven DeRosa, *Writing with Hitchcock: The Collaboration of Alfred Hitchcock and John Michael Hayes*. New York: Faber and Faber, 2001. xvi + 334 pp. $15 paper.

WALTER SREBNICK

Film studies has become more attentive to screenwriting and screenwriters than it once was. The work of directors canonized as auteurs a quarter of a century ago is now regarded less as the product of a single controlling vision and more as the result of creative collaboration, particularly between director and screenwriter. Some of the best Capra films, for example, are now also Riskin films; some of Ford's now also belong to Dudley Nichols. Given the resistance to depriving Hitchcock of what many now regard as an anachronistic stature among directors, it is not surprising that it has taken so long to assess and acknowledge the significance of his collaboration with screenwriters. The subject of Steven DeRosa's study, the working relationship of Hitchcock and John Michael Hayes, was perhaps a signature collaboration between a director and a writer. It began as a kind of mentorship, but ended in a bitter rift.

Interestingly, before Hayes scripted *Rear Window* (1954), *To Catch a Thief* (1955), *The Trouble With Harry* (1955), and *The Man Who Knew Too Much* (1956) at the beginning of what is arguably Hitchcock's most artistically productive decade (1953-63), the director had already worked in Hollywood with such writers as Thornton Wilder, Ben Hecht, Arthur Laurents, and Raymond Chandler. After Hayes, he collaborated with Maxwell Anderson, Samuel Taylor, Ernest Lehman, Joseph Stefano, Evan Hunter, Brian Moore, Jay Presson Allen, and Anthony Shaffer—also an impressive list. But only Hayes was to last four films with the demanding and mercurial director. Starting with this fact, DeRosa privileges the "Hayes films," arguing that they represent a special moment of artistic achievement in Hitchcock's career: a period of creative synergy and equipoise when he could employ his full technical arsenal to the richest advantage because he had

Hayes's creative gifts and life-affirming vision to work with. After the breach between the two, DeRosa argues that Hitchcock lost something he was never to recover.

Writing with Hitchcock is a valuable contribution to Hitchcock studies, one that breaks fresh ground. DeRosa provides a detailed and chronological narrative of the personal and working relationship of Hitchcock and Hayes during the period from 1953 to 1955, when the four films were produced. He systematically takes us through the collaboration of the two men on each of the films from the acquisition and adaptation of literary source materials, to the transformations from treatments to screenplays to shooting scripts, to accounts of the productions themselves. Some of the most interesting information concerns the challenges the writer faced in synchronizing his developing literary or verbal text with the director's plans for locations, individual shots, sequences, and with his overall visual conception. He argues that there was a special link between the two men that is evidenced in the interdependence of the screenplay with this visual conception. There are also interesting biographical sections on Hayes's career before and after Hitchcock and a parallel account of their lives and work. In addition, a long concluding chapter analyzes each of the screenplays, searching out the verbal and visual motifs in each.

Writing with Hitchcock draws heavily upon the author's extensive interviews with Hayes, who began his career as a radio writer. DeRosa also spoke with many of Hitchcock's associates from these years, and he uncovered new archival material. He begins the book with the screenwriter's hilarious account of the dinner at which the two met where the young Hayes tried desperately to sound sober and coherent as Hitchcock plied him with quantities of alcohol. Drinking heavily himself, Hitchcock didn't remember a word Hayes said, except that he liked that Hayes talked a lot, and he hired him.

Although there is much in the book that seems like familiar territory, much is also new. The problematic Hitchcock/Hayes relationship was first treated in Donald

Spoto's biography, *The Dark Side of Genius* (1982). But DeRosa describes the ongoing creative rapport between the two men and the steady demise of their pairing in much greater depth. There are also echoes of Spoto's critical perspective in *The Art of Alfred Hitchcock* (1977) in DeRosa's discussion of the themes of these films. Thomas Leitch's *Find the Director* (1991) and Lesley Brill's *The Hitchcock Romance* (1988) also influence DeRosa's reading of these works, particularly evident in DeRosa's assertions that the uniqueness of the Hayes films lies in the positive integration of the male protagonist within a larger community and in the possibility they hold out for redemptive love relationships. Clearly Robin Wood also has his impact on the author's approach.

There is, however, fascinating fresh material on how much Hayes was responsible for the genesis of the themes and characters of *Rear Window*, for example. We learn how the characters L.B. Jefferies and Lisa Fremont were based in part on the writer himself and his wife Mel, a fashion model, at the early stages of their relationship. Many of the issues Jeff and Lisa contend with in the film came out of the writer's own struggles with making a commitment to Mel while his career was still in flux, and with justifying his profession to Mel and his family. The new material on production work is also engaging, especially the discussion of the attempts to shoot *The Trouble With Harry* on location in Vermont, including at a makeshift sound stage in a local American Legion Barracks that doubled as a high-school gymnasium. There are also detailed accounts of working within and around production code censorship. How Hitchcock and Hayes got away with showing so much of Miss Torso's torso in *Rear Window* is one of the book's fascinating tidbits, as is the account of getting the censors to approve the suggestive dialogue between Cary Grant and Grace Kelly in *To Catch a Thief*. On the whole the technique was to write and shoot some scenes that Hitchcock knew the Production Code Administration would not approve, as a way of slipping through scenes he really wanted in the film as a compromise.

Beyond his very useful treatment of biographical and production material, DeRosa makes a case for what he calls the "Hayes touch" as the special element that defines these four films. This touch, he asserts, is conveyed in the writer's sophisticated dialogue and witty double entendres, such as when Grace Kelly observes in *To Catch a Thief* that Cary Grant and Brigitte Auber appear to be "conjugating irregular verbs" as they linger by a raft in the water of the Riviera; or when Shirley MacLaine cautions John Forsythe about her potential response to his romantic overtures by declaring that she has "a short fuse" in *The Trouble With Harry*. Another aspect of this touch, according to DeRosa, was Hayes's special skills at characterizing secondary figures, such as Stella in *Rear Window*, Mrs. Stevens in *To Catch a Thief*, and Mrs. Wiggs in *The Trouble With Harry*: outspoken and compelling women who help bring the audience together. DeRosa also lauds Hayes's ability to create tightly-constructed scripts that moved toward a clear and positive emotional resolution for the main characters at the same time that they build suspense, drop it, and then build it again to a crescendo.

But, most significantly, DeRosa argues, the Hayes signature grew out of the writer's own personal optimism and light touch, qualities that make these films among the most life-affirming that Hitchcock directed. They brought Hitchcock past a period of commercial failure in his post-Selznick years, thus reestablishing him at the box office. And, according to the author, they presented a lighter, ultimately comic vision of life in contrast to the darker, brooding films that came after them which had a tragic outlook and haunted male protagonists—*The Wrong Man* (1956), *Vertigo* (1958), *Psycho* (1959), and *The Birds* (1963).

Sadly, the relationship between Hitchcock and Hayes began to unravel as the writer's reputation grew during these two years. The director found it difficult to share the credit for these films with him. This is the down side of the story of this collaboration—Hitchcock's ego becoming threatened by what he seemed to regard as a challenge to his authorship. Things came apart after *The Man Who Knew Too Much*, when Hayes went to arbitration to thwart Hitchcock's intention to have his old friend Angus MacPhail (who had worked on the film's treatment and on an earlier version of the screenplay) share screen credit equally with the young writer. Hayes won, but the two never worked together again. Instead, an "unHitched" John Michael Hayes went on to a decade and a half of success at the top of his profession in Hollywood. But he was never again to script films on the artistic scale of *Rear Window*, nor was Hitchcock, in DeRosa's view, ever to regain "the touch."

As I indicated earlier, there is much valuable analysis and information in *Writing with Hitchcock* and much to admire. In its account of how Hayes adapted his literary sources for the screen, we get a clear understanding of the difference between visual and literary texts, and how much successfully writing the latter depended on the precise choice of images that both moved the plot forward and spoke to the larger themes of a film. Readers will be interested to learn just how much freedom Hitchcock allotted to Hayes and how much trust he placed in his skill and judgment. This was most fruitful in *Rear Window*, the most successful of their four joint efforts and the clearest case for considering the screenwriter indispensable to the authorship of the film. Hayes was responsible not only for dialogue, but for specific scenes, visual details, camera angles, and other such things. Yet DeRosa never slights Hitchcock's sense of total mastery of his craft, or the degree to which the whole experience of their collaboration was an education in film making for the writer.

What DeRosa does not provide is a theoretical framework for his treatment of authorship and film making. While the book is an excellent introduction to Hitchcock and to the process of cinematic creation, some might wish for less studio production detail and less retelling of the films themselves, and more theorizing about the connection between their verbal and visual texts. Many readers will also have trouble with DeRosa's clear preference for the wholesomeness of the male protagonists and relationships in these four films in contrast to the more problematic male figures and couples in some of Hitchcock's later work, such as *Vertigo* and *Psycho*. But because of its clarity of purpose, singleness of vision, and directness of approach, *Writing with Hitchcock* adds a welcome touch of critical freshness to the ongoing conversation about Hitchcock. It treats his films from the perspective of their creation and production, not from the several times removed posture and discourse of the academy. Because of this new perspective and DeRosa's veneration of the process of cinematic creation, few readers will be disappointed by *Working with Hitchcock*.

Peter Conrad, *The Hitchcock Murders*. London: Faber and Faber, 2000. 362 pp. $25.

CHARLES L.P. SILET

The cover photograph for *The Hitchcock Murders* is of an extreme close-up of a woman's mouth opened in a silent scream. In fact it is Janet Leigh's, playing Marion Crane, from the most famous scene in all of Hitchcock's *oeuvre*, the shower sequence from *Psycho* (1960). Peter Conrad begins his highly personal survey of Hitchcock's films—which he describes as "a voyage around the idiosyncratic universe" inside the director's head—with a memory of the day, an afternoon in 1961, when he solemnized his obsession with the director by playing hooky from school to see *Psycho* for the first time. Conrad confesses that at that screening he lost his innocence and discovered why the cinema existed: "to depict what you were not supposed to be looking at." The connections with *Psycho* are immediately obvious. The connections with Hitchcock's other films is what his book *The Hitchcock Murders* is all about.

If you think about it, and Peter Conrad has obviously thought about *all* of Hitchcock's films a lot, the screaming woman appears in many of the films: the unheard ones from the blondes murdered in *The Lodger*, the scream that turns into a train whistle in *The 39 Steps*, the strangled scream the camera backs away from in *Frenzy*, assorted screams in *Blackmail*, *To Catch a Thief*, *Rear Window*, and even Marion Crane's screams augmented by Bernard Herrmann's screeching score. The list is a long one. Women menaced, women scared, women killed, women just frightened by a mouse. Hitchcock filled his movies with screams. To make sense of the repeated images in Hitchcock's films, their origins, and the interpretation of them is the task Conrad has set himself. Using a "surrealistic association of ideas" and his own "brand of cinematic cross-cutting," which one might more accurately describe as "cultural" cross-cutting, he ranges backwards and forwards among Hitchcock's movies, touching on some of his television shows and isolated events from his life, with side-trips to discuss other filmmakers and their work, painters and their work, poets, musicians, writers (both screen and otherwise), and other creative arbiters of all kinds. As he notes in his preface, Conrad does not want to confine himself to examining only a half-dozen of the films the way he says most books on Hitchcock do; he wants to take the Master whole and he does. So Conrad's personal journey through Hitchcock's "head" ranges farther afield, as he writes on the earliest and perhaps superficially least characteristic of Hitchcock's silents, discusses such largely unexamined movies as *Jamaica Inn*, *Under Capricorn*, and *Mr. and Mrs. Smith*, and carefully considers the critically disparaged ones. *The Hitchcock Murders* pretty well covers the whole range of Hitchcock's creative output.

The book is divided into three main sections: "The Art of Murder," which "explores Hitchcock's daring as he prompts us to challenge legal and moral propriety"; "The Technique of Murder," which "shows him investigating the cinema's mechanical procedures and its remorseless execution of a world that, seen through a camera, is no longer safely, recognizably real"; and "The Religion of Murder," which "goes on to guess at Hitchcock's ulterior aim, and suggests that, by enticing us to look at death and to speculate about what follows it, he takes us into regions of experience that we can only call spiritual." Conrad does not follow—"plod" through, he calls it—Hitchcock's films chronologically because he believes that his concerns and tactics did not change "significantly over the course of a career that lasted half a century."

Conrad also announces in his preface that he will avoid the "theoretical controversies that vex and envenom the debate about Hitchcock in universities, where he is a pretext for trying out the conceptual tools deployed by queer polemics, feminism, post-structuralism, or whatever the latest methodological tic might be." And after a brief sample of an "embattled essay" on *Vertigo*, he wonders if the "conscientious axe-grinders," who only value the film as a field for theoretical play, have "paused to notice how deliriously beautiful and achingly sad it is?" "Luckily for Hitchcock," he concludes, "the world contains more lovers of film than pseudo-scientific professors of Film Studies."

Not surprisingly, given the personal, life-defining structure of the book, Conrad is a thoroughly "auteur" critic, even though he laments that the theory has probably gone out of fashion, "a casualty of those whimsical fads that academics call 'paradigm shifts.' " Conrad reads Hitchcock's films as the product of a "single, preemptory consciousness" imprinted on the "cinema's industrial artefacts," and concludes, "He had no doubts about the authorship of what he called 'a Hitchcock picture,' and nor do I." And just as Hitchcock's preoccupations, obsessions, and cultural experiences informed and shaped his films, so Conrad's journey through years of watching and thinking about the films and the director structures the book. Encountering Hitchcock has helped to define his personality and Conrad's odyssey is an attempt to discover how and to what end.

Although Conrad finds Hitchcock at the center of his films, he does not mean that they are "merely a record of obstinately personal anxieties and enmities." Rather Hitchcock through his films diagnosed "the discontents that chafe and rankle beneath the decorum of civilization" and "registered the phenomenological threat of an abruptly modernizing world." Hitchcock often wondered why people so eagerly wanted him to scare them. Terror, Conrad concludes, is the response "to an imminent revelation; it is the price exacted by dreams, which alarm us because they make visible what slumbers inside our heads." Hitchcock arouses our imagination and sets us free. Finally, *The Hitchcock Murders* is Peter Conrad's "grateful fan letter to the bogeyman."

The Hitchcock Murders is an absorbing, highly personal, quest through the world of Alfred Hitchcock, the man and the director of films. Combining forays into biography as well as autobiography, Conrad provides a narrative of cultural free association which ranges across much of the arts and history of western Europe. A sampling from the index under the letter "B" might provide an idea of his range: Béla Balázs, J.M. Barrie, Roland Barthes, Béla Bartók, Charles Baudelaire, André Bazin, Francis Breeding, Ludwig von Beethoven, Marie Adelaide Belloc Lowndes, Ingmar Bergman, George Berkeley, Franz Boas, Peter Bogdanovich, John Boorman, Margaret Bourke-White, Georges Braque, Bertold Brecht, André Breton, John Buchan, Luis Buñuel, and Edmund Burke. Within this broad cultural context Conrad provides readings for most of Hitchcock's individual films.

Because Conrad's range is so broad and his method so idiosyncratic, it is impossible to summarize his conclusions or to give an adequate idea of his text without actually replicating it. But a look at one of his inner-chapters may help. Under the heading of "The Philosophy of Motion" (pp. 167-81), he discusses motion or movement within the films, the "physics of film," as he describes it. Conrad begins with a truism: "Cinema is kinesis: it takes still pictures and makes them move." But the technical marvel of the illusion of movement provokes "a sense of unease," and the velocity of cinema, one of its pleasures, also produces a threat.

Under this general thesis Conrad launches into an analytical free fall. Picking up references to motion and the fear it has engendered, he shuttles from *Murder!* to *The Skin Game* and then from *Sabotage, Blackmail, The Ring,* to *Foreign Correspondent.* He plays off the title of Ethel Lina White's novel, *The Wheel Spins,* the source for *The Lady Vanishes,* into a discussion for several pages of that film, only to segue into a discussion of the example of the railway train Einstein employed for explaining his theory of relativity, which in turn leads him to look at the various train films Hitchcock directed: *Secret Agent, Strangers on a Train, The 39 Steps,* and *North by Northwest.* Conrad's observations on the model train used at the beginning of *The Lady Vanishes* gives way to a reference to Orson Welles, who, when he was making *Citizen Kane,* likened a movie studio to a train set. Without pause, Conrad comments on the miniature train set in the first version of *The Man Who Knew Too Much,* which then leads him to examine other modes of transport in *Foreign Correspondent* (flying), *Number Seventeen, Torn Curtain,* and *Secret Agent* (bus travel), finally lighting on a paragraph from A.S. Eddington's lectures on the behavior of time in *The Nature of the Physical World.* After he takes a detour to discuss Hitchcock's sedentary life and his fear of driving, Conrad pursues the reference to cars in *Rebecca* and *Psycho,* and the use of driving to mark sexual power in three Cary Grant films, *Suspicion, Notorious,* and *To Catch a Thief.* The ultimate film of movement, *North by Northwest,* is full of varying modes of travel, including planes, trains, buses, and automobiles, and it comes to resemble a film improvised on the run. Analyzing the actors, Cary Grant and Eva Marie Saint, generates a broader discussion of acting and star persona that includes James Mason and Martin Landau. This section of the book concludes where it began by returning to the idea of motion and fear, with references to *Spellbound, Secret Agent, Number Seventeen, The Lady Vanishes, Rear Window, Psycho,* and *Vertigo.*

Such a breathless combination of analysis, cultural references, and personal response characterizes the entire book. Surely no one has noticed so much detail in Hitchcock's films or made so much of it. In each chapter Conrad provides enough ideas and topics for a dozen or so longer essays. Nor has any other critic, to my mind at least, placed Hitchcock in such a wide range of cultural contexts. By doing so Conrad has written a book unique in Hitchcock studies.

Among the most interesting of Conrad's tactics is to provide an analysis of the films through an examination of the original source materials, the plays, short stories, and novels that Hitchcock routinely adapted for the screen. By discussing his sources Conrad can identify the traces the original material left behind in the adaptations. Such discussions tell us a lot about how Hitchcock's mind worked by highlighting what of the initial material he retained and what he omitted. This analysis is very valuable indeed.

By refusing to engage in the theoretical arguments generated by the academy critics, Conrad has spared his readers from the often convoluted prose and high contentiousness that usually goes along with such controversies. *The Hitchcock Murders* is written in an accessible style with wit and verve and is a pleasure to read, despite the author's occasional lapses into rather overheated prose.

The Hitchcock Murders, however, is not without its faults, and the primary one is the result of his overarching method. For all its exhilarating insights into the director and his films, it also produces frustration because it often lacks any sustained focus. The incessant jumping around tends to impede any sort of coherent understanding of the films individually. While it is clear why Conrad did not want to plod through the films chronologically, but rather approach them topically, reading the book can leave the reader with a feeling of disjunction, of reading a set of brilliant but scattered insights. Although taken as a whole Conrad's narrative constructs the trajectory of Hitchcock's career from journeyman filmmaker to visionary master, it is done so rather more obliquely than this reader, at least, could have wished.

There are also a few minor errors—for instance, does the dog actually "lunge" toward Farley Granger in *Strangers on a Train* before licking his hand?—but they are few and not particularly bothersome. Some readers may also quibble with some of Conrad's conclusions. For example, he does a lot with what he considers Hitchcock's substantial debt to surrealism; one might wonder if he overdoes this a bit. And was Hitchcock as anti-sound and anti-color as Conrad suggests? Also, Conrad's militantly anti-academic stance does not do justice to the wide range of critical commentary written over a considerable period of time by many thoughtful professors of Film Studies. Surely Conrad has looked at what others have written about Hitchcock and some of that must be present in his book, although the lack of any bibliography or endnotes prevents any attribution or acknowledgment. Fortunately, the book has a comprehensive index.

The Hitchcock Murders is a welcome new book. And Conrad's attempt to read Hitchcock's work as one continuous film has its payoffs. Tying the various films together in the way he does proves well worth the reading. There is so much here and it is presented so much sensitivity and seriousness that, if it is still necessary at this late date, once again we are reminded of the talent and genius of one of the cinema's most important and influential makers of film.

Susan Smith, *Hitchcock: Suspense, Humour and Tone*. London: British Film Institute, 2000. xiii + 162 pp. $24.95 paper.

JOE MCELHANEY

For a book of a modest 154 pages in length, the stated intentions of Susan Smith's *Hitchcock: Suspense, Humour and Tone* are quite ambitious. In a brief introduction, she notes that many of Hitchcock's films "operate on the basis of direct address" (p. vii) in which a strong authorial sensibility manifests itself, one strongly marked by its mixture of suspense and humor. The aim of the book, strongly focused on the elusive problem of tone, "is to arrive at a more composite sense of what the process of watching a Hitchcock movie entails" (p. xi). Five chapters follow this introduction, the first and last devoted to a close study of a single film, *Sabotage* and *The Birds* respectively. In between, there are individual chapters on suspense, humor, and *mise-en-scène*. Since much of what is important about Smith's study is contained in the second and third chapters, I will begin there.

In spite of Hitchcock's frequent declarations on surprise being antithetical to suspense, Smith persuasively argues in her second chapter that surprise is fundamental to Hitchcock's cinema and "often becomes an epistemic precondition for some of the most intense, important forms of suspense" (p. 41). Throughout this strong chapter, Smith outlines the relationship between surprise and suspense and the key role of suppressive information, all of which are analyzed in relation to smaller localized methods of narration and larger overarching structures. There is also a useful breakdown here of Hitchcock's approach to suspense in terms of three forms of address: vicarious, shared, and direct. Smith relies rather too exclusively on the Truffaut book for Hitchcock's statements on the supposed distinction between surprise and suspense, a distinction which he elsewhere expressed in different terms, fully allowing for the possibility of surprise as a significant component of his work. (Hitchcock's 1949 essay, "The Enjoyment of Fear," easily available in the

Hitchcock on Hitchcock collection, should have been drawn upon. Here he writes of the complex relationship between suspense and surprise, or what he termed "terror.") Still, there is much in this chapter to value.

The primary emphasis in the third chapter is on the interdependent relationship between humor and suspense, with *Rope* serving as a central text, particularly for the ways in which it revolves around the question of humor in relation to violence and death. Given the extent to which the aptness or inaptness of finding humor in the film's subject matter is also a running debate expressed by some of the characters in *Rope*, Smith's choice could scarcely be more felicitous. The writing here is livelier than in the preceding sections of the book and produces some of Smith's best insights, as in the parallels she draws between Herb and Joe in *Shadow of a Doubt* and Philip and Brandon in *Rope*. She notes, for example, that the comic scenario at work in a minor key in *Shadow of a Doubt* becomes the central thrust of the scenario to *Rope*, with Herb and Joe functioning as embryonic versions of Brandon and Rupert. Indeed, the chapter as a whole gains much of its strength from Smith's exploration of the neglected topic of humor in Hitchcock.

But if this is the liveliest section of the book, it is also the one in which the weaknesses of the hermetic nature of Smith's analysis are especially apparent. The book would have benefitted by a certain broadening of horizons, exploring ways in which Hitchcock's cinema was engaging in a dialogue not simply with other Hitchcock films but with the culture *surrounding* those films as well. Smith is doubtless correct in her emphasis on what she calls "tonal antithesis" in relation to humor and violence in Hitchcock. But she never addresses the question of where the sensibility in the films comes from, culturally or historically, in spite of the fact that this bold contrast in tone between deadpan comedy and extreme violence is part of a tradition of English black humor. This in turn arises out of an overall fascination with contrast and counterpoint, a fascination that Hitchcock himself was well aware of, often discussed, and may be seen as part of the history of English thought. Furthermore, if this slippage between the comic and thriller elements in Hitchcock "contributes substantially to dislodging the security of the viewer's position" (p. 49), then why were so many of these films popular with audiences and why do they continue to exert their fascination with spectators today in a way that very few films of the same period are able to match? Asking herself questions of this nature might have allowed Smith to avoid the repetition of terms like "subversive" and "radical" in describing Hitchcock's approach to everything from gender issues to narrative structures while often failing to adequately define what the films are being subversive of and what they are radical in relation to.

In the following chapter, dealing with *mise-en-scène*, Smith insists upon the importance of paying greater attention to issues of space and decor in Hitchcock while also outlining some significant ways in which the point-of-view shot operates outside of character identification. She writes that what is being offered is "a fresh look" (p. 76) at this topic. But the chapter is flawed by technical inaccuracies and misdescriptions: it is not a "zoom-in device" (p. 81) when Gay spots Mrs. Paradine in the witness box in *The Paradine Case* but a downward movement of the crane; it is not a "track-in" (p. 100) to Mrs. Bates's bronzed hands in *Psycho* but a zoom. In both cases, these movements have very definite functions which they assume in the films and to misdescribe them misses their point, particularly problematic in a chapter which claims to offer a "fresh look."

Furthermore, this chapter is hampered by a tendency to interpret certain aspects of Hitchcock's *mise-en-scène* in a highly questionable manner. For example, Smith finds "serenity and composure" in the crossed hands of the bronze casting in Mrs. Bates's room and argues that the laced cuffs suggest "a woman of delicate, sophisticated taste," all of this pointing to an "alternative female realm" which resists male control (p. 100). But does it? The fact that the hands are bronzed may suggest a form of embalming as much as it does tenderness; that the hands are severed from the body of the mother may connote violence against her as much as it does her "non-verbal challenge" to male discourses; and the crude abruptness of the *zoom* into these hands completes this aspect of latent violence. My concern here is not simply to express that I disagree with Smith in the way that she is reading this shot. Rather, the nature of this reading fails to follow through on Smith's claim that her book offers a "more composite sense of what the experience of watching a Hitchcock movie entails." What is offered here is not a careful act of criticism and commentary which traces out this composite sense of the experience of watching the film but a pre-determined reading that feels imposed.

If this were the only moment when such a questionable interpretation arose then it would be a minor point. But, in fact, interpretations of this nature dominate much of the book, especially the first and last chapters, when Smith's propensity for reading Hitchcock's cinema allegorically is at its strongest. At the center of the first chapter is the argument that *Sabotage* represents "one of the most fascinating self-reflections upon the nature of Hitchcock's *own* cinema" (p. 3). Central here is the controversial sequence in which Stevie is killed by a terrorist bomb. Hitchcock later came to regret having filmed the sequence in the way that he had, in building up an enormous amount of anxiety on the part of the viewer for nearly fifteen minutes and then not relieving this with Stevie's rescue. Rather than following Hitchcock's lead, Smith reads Hitchcock's own declarations about the sequence being an example of "bad technique" as attempts to distance himself from the more disturbing implications of his own practices. I agree with Smith that the bomb sequence does not completely violate the overall logic of *Sabotage*, in which the death of Stevie is simply a fulfillment of the film's basic drives. But aside from the book's positioning of *Sabotage* as an exemplary rather than eccentric Hitchcock work, I have two major difficulties in fully accepting her approach.

The first is that it is based on a reading of the film in which Verloc, as combined cinema proprietor and saboteur, assumes the role of a negative double or surrogate for Hitchcock. This claim is backed up with numerous bits of evidence, from Verloc's failed act of sabotage resulting in the lights of London going out (which Smith reads as an analogy for the way that Hitchcock "often plunges *his* audiences into darkness, both literally and metaphorically" [p. 3]) to the package that Verloc gives to Stevie to carry across London and that includes reels of a film called *Bartholomew the Strangler*, a title that "could easily belong to the Hitchcock thriller genre" (p. 6). As allegorical readings go, this has a certain power. But she gets carried away with her own interpretive skills and sees doubles for Hitchcock in a number of unlikely areas. She draws upon wordplay and rhyming effects in Verloc's visit to the professor's shop in which we hear a "*cock*erel" (p. 6) crowing and finds spectacular relations between Hitchcock, Verloc, and Cock Robin in the "Who Killed Cock Robin?" sequence. The death of the bird in the Disney cartoon becomes "an act of authorial suicide or self-castration" in which we find a "killing-off of the 'cock' in 'Hitchcock' " (p. 12) while at the same moment Hitchcock asserts his own authorial power over Verloc by disposing of him in the sequence immediately following this. At moments such as these, Smith's allegorical methods give way to a form of interpretive delirium.

Equally problematic is her reading of Stevie as a latent serial killer or psychopath on the order of Uncle Charlie or Bruno Anthony. Stevie's statement to Ted that he has seen *Bartholomew the Strangler* fourteen times leads Smith to argue that what we have are "rather ominous, early signs of the boy's own compulsive absorption with violence" (p. 9), hence the B (as in Bartholomew) on his cap as well as Ted and the bus conductor's playful reference to Stevie as Bartholomew. In killing Stevie off, Smith believes that it is as if Hitchcock wanted to "stop this embryonic version of a Hitchcock villain" (p. 9). Yet a central problem with the bomb sequence, as Hitchcock and Truffaut discussed, was that audiences had built up a strong degree of sympathy for Stevie. The film had gone to such lengths to paint him as endearing and childlike even before he was given the bomb that to put the audience through an emotional ringer and then not grant them a release from this state provoked an understandable resentment. For a book so concerned with the question of tone, then, Smith has difficulty in getting a firm handle on the tone of this particular sequence.

The final chapter on *The Birds* returns the book full circle to the opening in its strategy of close analysis of a single film. At the beginning of this chapter, she aptly notes that the film's refusal to supply any form of conventional explanation for the attacks becomes a way of ''challenging our more habitual expectations'' as the film encourages us to ''adopt a more composite, meaningful outlook upon its narrative world'' (p. 127). It would have been refreshing had Smith taken this opportunity to challenge and extend some of her own methods. Instead, the chapter serves as a moment of culmination for the interpretive strategies present throughout the rest of the text in which precise meanings are assigned to some very complex images. There is a return to the notion of the double or surrogate for Hitchcock. Here that double is Mitch (rhymes with Hitch). Again there are boldly argued but unconvincing readings of key moments in the film. One example: The birds in the final shot are massing for Mitch since it is ''*his* personal journey that is now beginning'' (p. 148). And inaccuracies and distortions in shot descriptions reappear as an extension of the book's extreme interpretive methods. In the birdshop sequence, the ''motif of encagement'' (p. 148) is not associated with Mitch in the way that she maintains. The frame blow-up that is designed to illustrate this is lifted out of a fast tracking shot as Mitch and Melanie are walking across the shop and is not even noticeable in the film as it is being projected. And so on. The result of this type of reading is that Hitchcock emerges as an artist of virtually unrivaled authority and power, a metaphoric figure insinuating himself into the body of his work at all formal levels while also miraculously making films that overthrow or subvert dominant viewing strategies and social discourses.

Susan Smith has focused on some important aspects of Hitchcock's cinema. Her approach to humor and issues of suspense offers much that will be of value to future Hitchcock scholarship. But the need to interpret in a "brilliant" manner limits this enormously promising and often boldly argued book.

Martin Grams, Jr., and Patrik Wikstrom, *The Alfred Hitchcock Presents Companion*. Churchville, Maryland: OTR Publishing, 2001. 656 pp. $35 paper.

SIDNEY GOTTLIEB

Hitchcock's work in other media besides film is a relatively uncharted frontier ready for exploration by scholars. Just about everyone, of course, knows about Hitchcock's involvement with the long-running television show that carried his name and was largely responsible—even more than his films—for imprinting his voice, image, and darkly comic persona onto public consciousness, and for giving him a level of financial return rare among directors. (I avoid using the terms financial "independence" or "security" because I am not sure that Hitchcock's wealth brought him either: in some ways, various tensions in his creative process increased rather than disappeared when instead of doing battle with corporations he in effect became the corporation.) But we need to know more about the details of this involvement: perhaps especially about the twenty television dramas that he directed, because of our continuing interest in that kind of "authorship," but also about other aspects of his activities as producer, advisor, consultant, and investor in the series, as well as his role as one of the artifacts constructed, presented, and marketed by the shows.

The Alfred Hitchcock Presents Companion, by Martin Grams, Jr., and Patrik Wikstrom contains an enormous amount of material on Hitchcock's activities apart from his role as a film director. The bulk of the book is taken up with a meticulous index of all the episodes on the various television series Hitchcock was associated with, including broadcast dates, source of the screenplay, cast and crew credits, a detailed synopsis of the episode, a transcription of Hitchcock's opening and closing comments, and miscellaneous information. The authors tacitly acknowledge that much of their interest lies in this last category, disarmingly labeled "trivia," and they include such things as production anecdotes, quotations from people involved in the shows, cross-references among episodes, selections from reviews, and details about other work done by various members of the cast, crew, or writing staff.

Much of the material in the book reflects the authors' interest not only in Hitchcock but in everything connected with everything connected with Hitchcock, and this principle of inclusion may charm some readers and frustrate others. One is just as likely to come across a detailed description of director Arthur Hiller's godmother's comments on her visit to the studio set (p. 297)—she is more puzzled than amused, although always proud of her godson, we find out—as a mini-essay on the Hitchcock-directed episode "Arthur" and some patient investigative work on the mysterious author of the original story on which the screenplay was based (pp. 274-75). And the book moves progressively away from Hitchcock the creative and at least supervisory person to "Hitchcock" the brand-name and artifact: following the detailed section on the original episodes of *Alfred Hitchcock Presents* and the *Alfred Hitchcock Hour* is an extensive treatment of the new version of the show televised during the 1980s, which included recycled Hitchcock comments and remade versions of some original episodes as well as newly scripted shows; and all this is followed by nearly fifty pages on anthologies of stories that came out under Hitchcock's name: not just the *Stories They Wouldn't Let Me Do On TV* variety but also the many children's books. At this point, I feel that we are closer to losing than finding Hitchcock.

The anthologies and the remakes of the television shows do indeed tell us something useful about the reception and "afterlife" of Hitchcock's work and persona. But I suspect that in most copies of this book, the concluding sections will not be nearly as thumbed-through as the invaluable middle section on the original series and the extensive introduction, telling how Hitchcock came to television, with particularly interesting sections on his collaboration with Joan Harrison and Norman Lloyd, his radio work, the television episodes he directed (covered in an essay by Ulrich Rüdel, one of several contributors to the volume besides Grams and Wikstrom), and alternate versions of his introductory and concluding remarks on various shows. All this is interspersed with rare photos and illustrations of Hitchcock and comments on the dissemination of the Hitchcock name and image via board games, record albums, sheet music, Absolut vodka ads, and repeated references in *MAD Magazine* and animated cartoons.

If I sometimes seem impatient with the centrifugal energy of Grams and Wikstrom, I should add that this far-ranging, miscellaneous quality makes the book a fascinating "companion": not a book that one is likely to read through sequentially from cover to cover, with equal interest in all its parts, but certainly one worth wandering in and consulting at length, filled with details and quotations of material often unavailable elsewhere that will serve a variety of purposes and pleasures, including scholarly ones. From beginning to end, *The Alfred Hitchcock Companion Presents Companion* is overflowing with Hitchcock and things Hitchcockian, and if it enthusiastically traverses the high and the low, the sublime and the ridiculous, the centers and the margins, this may be necessary to take the full measure of the worlds envisioned, created, and otherwise imprinted by Hitchcock.

INDEX TO *HITCHCOCK ANNUAL*
1992-2001

ARTICLES

Watts, Stephen, Alfred Hitchcock on Music in Films, an interview, introduction by Margaret Anne O'Connor (1994), 149-57.

Working with Hitch: A Screenwriter's Forum with Evan Hunter, Arthur Laurents, and Joseph Stefano, by Walter Srebnick (2001-02), 1-37.

Writing for Hitch: An Interview with Evan Hunter, by Charles L.P. Silet (1995-96), 117-26.

REVIEWS

Allen, Richard and S. Ishii-Gonzalès, eds., *Alfred Hitchcock: Centenary Essays*, rev. by James Castonguay (2000-01), 174-82.

Apter, Emily and William Pietz, eds., *Fetishism as Cultural Discourse*, rev. by Diane Carson (1995-96), 137-47.

Arrowsmith, William, *Antonioni: The Poet of Images*, rev. by Christopher Brookhouse (1995-96), 164.

Auiler, Dan, *Hitchcock's Notebooks: An Authorized and Illustrated Look Inside the Creative Mind of Alfred Hitchcock*, rev. by Charles L.P. Silet (1999-2000), 171-73.

Baylor, Jeffrey, rev. of Michael Sevastakis, *Songs of Love and Death: The Classical American Horror Film of the 1930s* (1995-96), 134-36.

Bloch, Robert, *Psycho*, rev. by Charles L.P. Silet (1999-2000), 166-68.

Boyd, David, ed., *Perspectives on Alfred Hitchcock*, rev. by Christopher Brookhouse (1995-96), 163.

Bowman, Barbara, *Master Space: Film Images of Capra, Lubitsch, Sternberg, and Wyler*, rev. by Leland Poague (1993), 132-36.

Brill, Lesley, rev. of Stephen Rebello, *Alfred Hitchcock and the Making of* Psycho (1992), 144-50.

Brookhouse, Christopher, rev. of William Arrowsmith, *Antonioni: The Poet of Images* (1995-96), 164.

_____, rev. of David Boyd, ed., *Perspectives on Alfred Hitchcock* (1995-96), 163.

_____, rev. of Joan Copjec, ed., *Shades of Noir* (1995-96), 162-63.

_____, rev. of Neil P. Hurley, *Soul in Suspense: Hitchcock's Fright and Delight* (1993), 157-61.

_____, rev. of Helen Keyssar, *Robert Altman's America* (1992), 161-63.

_____, rev. of Glenn Man, ed., *Radical Visions: American Film Renaissance, 1967-1976* (1995-96), 163-64.

Contributors

Richard Allen is Associate Professor of Cinema Studies at New York University. He is author of *Projecting Illusion* (Cambridge, 1995) and co-editor of *Film Theory and Philosophy* (Clarendon Press, 1997), *Alfred Hitchcock: Centenary Essays* (BFI, 1999), and *Wittgenstein, Theory and the Arts* (Routledge, 2001). He is currently writing a book on Hitchcock for Cambridge University Press.

Sarah Berry is the author of *Screen Style: Fashion and Femininity in 1930s Hollywood* (University of Minnesota Press). She writes on film, media, and cultural studies, and designs interactive multimedia. She teaches film studies at Portland State University in Portland, Oregon.

Paula Marantz Cohen, Distinguished Professor of English at Drexel University, is the author of five books, including *Alfred Hitchcock: The Legacy of Victorianism* and, most recently, *Silent Film and the Triumph of the American Myth* (Oxford University Press, 2001). She is currently working on a book on John Singer Sargent and his circle.

Marshall Deutelbaum teaches courses in film and film theory in the English Department at Purdue University.

Sidney Gottlieb is Professor of English at Sacred Heart University, Fairfield, Connecticut. His collection of interviews with Hitchcock is forthcoming from the University of Mississippi Press.

Sam Ishii-Gonzalès is a doctoral candidate in Cinema Studies at New York University. He is the co-editor of *Alfred Hitchcock: Centenary Essays* (BFI, 1999) and *Hitchcock Past and Future* (Routledge, forthcoming). His dissertation considers the works of Fassbinder, Pasolini, and Warhol in relation to Deleuze's semiotics of film.

Adrian Martin, Honorary Senior Research Fellow at the Victorian College of the Arts (Australia), is the author of *Once*

Upon a Time in America (BFI, 1998) and *Phantasms* (Penguin, 1994). He is film critic for *The Age* (Melbourne) and co-editor of *Senses of Cinema* (www.sensesofcinema.com). He is currently completing a book on Terrence Malick.

Joe McElhaney is currently Visiting Assistant Professor of Film Studies at Hunter College.

Steven Jay Schneider is a Ph.D. candidate in Cinema Studies at New York University. He is co-editor of *Dark Thoughts: Philosophic Reflections on Cinematic Horror* (Scarecrow Press, forthcoming) and author of "Manufacturing Horror in Hitch- cock's *Psycho*" (*CineAction* no. 50, 1999).

Charles L.P. Silet teaches courses in film and modern literature at Iowa State University. His books include *Oliver Stone: Interviews* (University of Mississippi Press) and a forthcoming collection of critical essays on Steven Spielberg.

Walter Srebnick was one of the coordinators of the 1999 NYU Hitchcock Centennial Conference. He is co-editor of *Hitch- cock's Rereleased Films: From* Rope *to* Vertigo (Wayne State University Press, 1991).

Constantine Verevis teaches in the School of Literary, Visual, and Performance Studies at Monash University, Melbourne. He is presently developing a project on cinematic remaking.

James M. Vest is Professor of French at Rhodes College in Memphis, Tennessee, where he teaches in the Inter- disciplinary Humanities program. He is the author of several articles and books on French literature and culture. His essays on Hitchcock's French connections have appeared in the *Hitchcock Annual*, *Journal of the Midwest Modern Language Association*, and *The French Review*. His book *Hitchcock and France* is forthcoming from Praeger.